**THE GRAMMAR OF ENGLISH PREDICATE
COMPLEMENT CONSTRUCTIONS**

THE GRAMMAR OF ENGLISH PREDICATE COMPLEMENT CONSTRUCTIONS

Peter S. Rosenbaum

RESEARCH MONOGRAPH No. 47

THE M.I.T. PRESS, CAMBRIDGE, MASSACHUSETTS

Copyright © 1967 by
Peter S. Rosenbaum

Set by ⋃NEOPRINT *and printed and bound in the United States*
of America by The Riverside Press

Library of Congress catalog card number: 67-27350

To my grandparents
Isidore and Jennie Weiss

Foreword

This is the forty-seventh volume in the M.I.T. Research Monograph Series published by The M.I.T. Press. The objective of this series is to contribute to the professional literature a number of significant pieces of research, larger in scope than journal articles but normally less ambitious than finished books. We believe that such studies deserve a wider circulation than can be accomplished by informal channels, and we hope that this form of publication will make them readily accessible to research organizations, libraries, and independent workers.

Howard W. Johnson

Preface

This book originated as a doctoral dissertation prepared at M.I.T. during 1964–1965. Certain of the conclusions drawn in the work have been called into question by recent findings. First, the number of clear cases of verb phrase complementation has diminished to the point where their general existence becomes questionable. (The Appendix, which provides verb classifications, is correspondingly unreliable.) Second, the pronoun replacement transformation, which, in this work, is dependent upon the structure created by the prior application of the extraposition transformation, now appears to be an independent transformation ordered prior to extraposition which generates a surface structure distinctly different from that generated by extraposition. Third, noun phrase complements containing the "POSS-ing" complementizer undergo pronoun replacement, a finding which supersedes the present work's implied limitation of pronoun replacement to noun phrase complements containing the "for-to" complementizer. Fourth, new data indicate that the proposed distribution of complementizers, which distinguishes the "POSS-ing" and "for-to" complementizers from the "that" complementizer, is not wholly correct. Fifth, it is now clear that the grammar of embedded sentences must be expanded so as to provide for question sentences as noun phrase complements. Finally, the present work, with no justification, assumes the validity of the cyclic principle, which governs the application of many of the proposed transformational rules. Recent research suggests that empirical evidence supporting this principle is extremely scanty and dubious, a circumstance which indicates the potential necessity to reformulate and to reorder certain of the transformational rules considered at present to operate cyclically. These topics are the subject of much current syntactic research. Regardless of outcome, the present work provides a descriptive introduction to the study of abstract syntax and to the general problems of complex sentence formation which a linguistic description must resolve.

Throughout the text, the terms "underlying structure" and "superficial structure" correspond, respectively, to the now more familiar terms "deep structure" and "surface structure."

The author wishes to express his gratitude to Noam Chomsky and Paul Postal who, giving freely of their time, influenced virtually every aspect of this book. The author has also profited from many discussions of English grammar with Edward Klima, Thomas Bever, Bruce Fraser, Barbara Hall Partee, George Lakoff, Terence Langendoen, John Ross, and Arnold Zwicky. The author is grateful to the U.S. Office of Education for providing fellowships funds, under Title IV of the National Defense Education Act, which enabled him to pursue graduate study in linguistics at M.I.T. and to the IBM Corporation for its support of the author's preliminary study of predicate complementation in English during the summer months of 1964.

Yorktown Heights, New York
May 1967   *Peter S. Rosenbaum*

Contents

THE GRAMMAR OF ENGLISH PREDICATE COMPLEMENT CONSTRUCTIONS

1. The Results of the Inquiry

The aim of the present study is to develop an adequate framework for
describing certain types of sentential complementation in English. In
particular, this study deals with instances where sentences are embedded
in noun phrases (henceforth noun phrase complementation) and in verb
phrases (verb phrase complementation). In terms of the theory of syntax developed by Chomsky in his Aspects of the Theory of Syntax,[1] the
descriptive apparatus postulated to explain noun phrase and verb phrase
complementation consists of, first, a set of phrase structure rewriting
rules that generate underlying sentence structures and, second, a set of
transformational rules that map underlying structures onto new derived
structures. The various considerations brought to bear in this study
lead to the conclusion that an adequate description of noun phrase and
verb phrase complementation contains the phrase structure and transformational rules summarized in the following pages.

1.1 Phrase Structure Rules

Operating in conjunction with two basic rules that expand S (sentence)
and PDP (predicate phrase) into NP, AUX, PDP, and VP, ADV, respectively, the two phrase structure rules that are central to the complement
systems under discussion can be stated as follows:

PS Rule 1   VP $\longrightarrow$ V   (NP)   (PP) $\begin{Bmatrix} S \\ PP \end{Bmatrix}$

PS Rule 2   NP $\longrightarrow$ DET   N   (S)

These two phrase structure rules allow for the generation of a variety of underlying structures. Most pertinent to the present study are the following seven structures:[2]

(1)

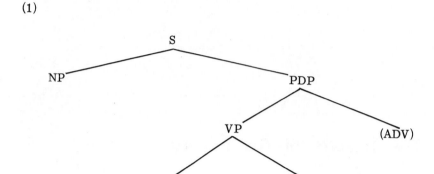

The underlying structure (1), an instance of <u>intransitive verb phrase complementation</u>, is generated as the result of the particular application of PS Rule 1, which expands VP into V, S.

(2)

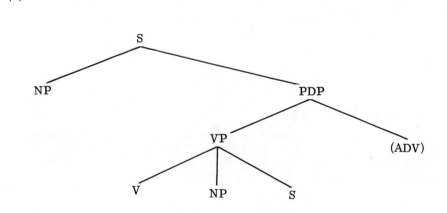

The application of PS Rule 1, in which VP is expanded as V, NP, S, yields instances of <u>transitive verb phrase complementation</u> as shown in (2).

(3)

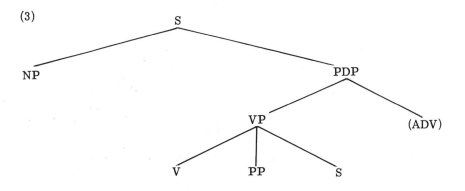

Where VP is expanded into V, PP, S, PS Rule 1 generates instances of <u>oblique verb phrase complementation</u>, in (3).

(4)

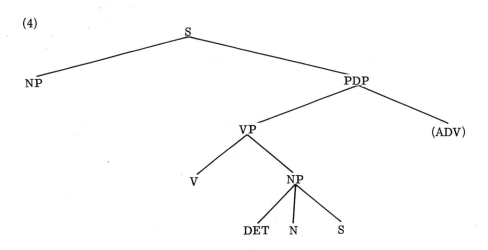

The underlying structure diagramed in (4), an instance of <u>object noun phrase complementation</u>, requires the application of PS Rule 1 through which VP is expanded into V, NP, and the application of PS Rule 2 to this NP (henceforth the <u>underlying object NP</u>).

(5)

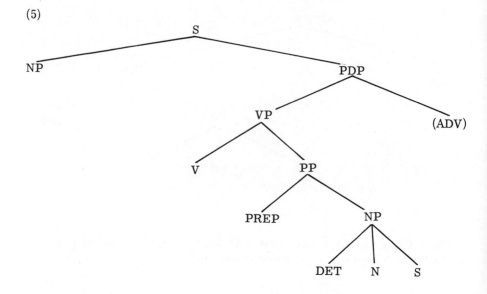

When PS Rule 2 is applied to the NP produced through the application of PS Rule 2, which expands VP into V, PP, the grammar generates instances of <u>intransitive oblique noun phrase complementation</u>, as in (5).

(6)

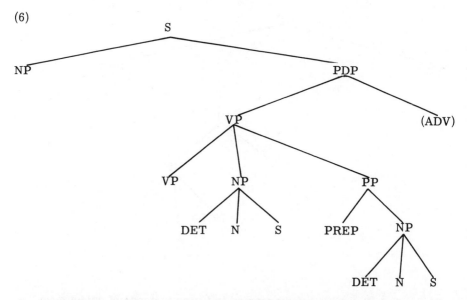

The expansion of VP into V, NP, PP permits the generation of instances of <u>transitive oblique noun phrase complementation</u>, shown in (6). In this case, the underlying object NP may be expanded by PS Rule 2 along with the NP dominated by PP.

(7)

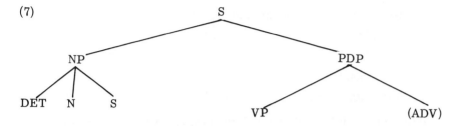

Since the phrase structure expanding S yields NP, AUX, VP, PS Rule 2 may apply to the NP in this configuration (henceforth the underlying sub-ject NP) to generate instances of subject noun phrase complementation, given in (7).

1.2 Transformational Rules

PS Rules 1 and 2 suffice to generate the most central structures under-lying noun phrase and verb phrase complementation (predicate comple-mentation collectively) in English. The transformational rules necessary to the generation of appropriate derived structures are given in this sec-tion. These rules are strictly ordered, apply cyclically, and are obliga-tory unless otherwise marked.

1. Complementizer Placement Transformation—T_{CP}

   A. $\quad$ X $\qquad$ N $\qquad$ [NP + Y]$_S$ $\qquad\qquad$ Z
      $\qquad\qquad\quad$ [−D]

   $\qquad$ 1 $\qquad$ 2 $\qquad\qquad$ 3 $\qquad\qquad\qquad$ 4 $\Longrightarrow$

   $\qquad$ 1, 2, [−D]+3, 4

   B. $\quad$ X $\qquad$ N $\qquad$ NP + PDP $\qquad\qquad$ Z
      $\qquad\qquad\quad \begin{bmatrix} +D \\ \alpha E \end{bmatrix}$

   $\qquad$ 1 $\qquad$ 2 $\qquad\qquad$ 3 $\qquad\qquad\qquad$ 4 $\Longrightarrow$

   $\qquad$ 1, 2, $\begin{bmatrix} +D \\ \alpha E \end{bmatrix}$+3, 4

   C. $\quad$ X $\qquad$ V $\qquad$ (NP) $\;$ NP + PDP $\qquad$ Z
      $\qquad\qquad\quad \begin{bmatrix} +D \\ \alpha E \end{bmatrix}$

   $\qquad$ 1 $\qquad$ 2 $\qquad$ 3 $\qquad$ 4 $\qquad\qquad\qquad$ 5 $\Longrightarrow$

   $\qquad$ 1, 2, 3, $\begin{bmatrix} +D \\ \alpha E \end{bmatrix}$+4, 5

   D. $\quad$ X $\qquad \begin{bmatrix} +D \\ \alpha E \end{bmatrix}$ $\quad$ NP $\quad \begin{Bmatrix} V \\ \text{have} \\ \text{be} \end{Bmatrix}$ $\qquad$ + Y

   $\qquad$ 1 $\qquad$ 2 $\qquad\qquad$ 3 $\qquad\qquad\qquad$ 4 $\Longrightarrow$

   $\qquad$ 1, 2, 3, 2 + 4

2. Identity Erasure Transformation—T_{IE}

W	(NP)	X	+D	NP	Y	(NP)	Z
1	2	3	4	5	6	7	8

(i)[3] 5 is erased by 2

(ii) 5 is erased by 7

The following conditions (henceforth the <u>erasure principle</u>) govern the application of the identity erasure transformation. An NP_j is erased by an identical NP_i if and only if there is a S_α such that

  (i) NP_j is dominated by S_α

  (ii) NP_i neither dominates nor is dominated by S_α

  (iii) for all NP_k neither dominating nor dominated by S_α, the distance between NP_j and NP_k is greater than the distance between NP_j and NP_i where the distance between two nodes is defined in terms of the number of branches in the path connecting them.

3. Subject-Object Inversion Transformation—T_{SOI}

X	NP	AUX	V [+SOI]	NP	S	Y
1	2	3	4	5	6	7 $\Longrightarrow$

1, 5, 3, 4, 6, to +2, 7

4. Passive Transformation—T_P (usually optional)

X	NP	AUX	V	(PREP)	NP	by + P	Y	
1	2	3	4	5	6	7	8	9 $\Longrightarrow$

1, 6, 3, 4, 5, $\emptyset$, 7, 2, 9

5. Extraposition Transformation—T_E (usually optional)

X	N $\begin{bmatrix} +\text{PRO} \\ \text{NOT} \begin{bmatrix} +\text{D} \\ +\text{E} \end{bmatrix} \end{bmatrix}$	S	Y
1	2	3	4 $\Longrightarrow$

1, 2, $\emptyset$, 4+3

6. Optional Complementizer Deletion Transformation—T_{OCD} (usually optional)

X	$\begin{Bmatrix} V \\ ADJ \end{Bmatrix}$				NP	Y
		a.	N [+PRO]	[+D]		
		b.	(NP)	[−D]		
1	2		3	4	5	6 $\Longrightarrow$

1, 2, 3, $\emptyset$, 5, 6

7.　Auxiliary Transformation—T_{AUX}[4]

X	Af	v	Y
1	2	3	4 $\Longrightarrow$

(in particular where Af is [+E] and v is V, <u>have</u>, <u>be</u>, or NP)

$1, \emptyset, 3+2, 4$

8.　Pronoun Replacement Transformation—T_{PR}

X	N [+PRO] NP	(AUX	$\left\{\begin{array}{c} \text{V} \\ \text{be ADJ} \\ \text{[+PR]} \end{array}\right\}$	(MAN))	[+D]	NP	Y
1	2	3	4	5	6	7	8 $\Longrightarrow$

$1, 7, 3, 4, 5, 6, \emptyset, 8$

9.　Pronoun Deletion Transformation—T_{PD}

X	N [+PRO]	$\left\{\begin{array}{ll} a. & \emptyset \\ b. & \text{ADV} \end{array}\right\}$	S	Y
1	2	3	4	5 $\Longrightarrow$

(a. has a few exceptions)
(b. is usually optional)

$1, \emptyset, 3, 4, 5$

In addition to the transformational rules just defined there are several others that are partially ordered. The most essential of these are the preposition deletion transformation, which must precede the pronoun replacement transformation, and the obligatory complementizer deletion transformation, which must follow the pronoun replacement transformation.

10.　Preposition Deletion Transformation—T_{PPD}

X	PREP	$\left[\begin{array}{c} \text{N} \\ \left[\begin{array}{c} \text{[+PRO]} \\ \left\{\begin{array}{c} \text{[-D]} \\ \text{[-E]} \end{array}\right\} \end{array}\right] \end{array}\right]$	Y
1	2	3	4 $\Longrightarrow$

$1, \emptyset, 3, 4$

11.　Obligatory Complementizer Deletion Transformation—T_{CD}

X	[+C]	VP	Y
1	2	3	4 $\Longrightarrow$

$1, \emptyset, 3, 4$

The discussion to follow will explore the justification of both the rules and their ordering in the description of predicate complementation in English. In the course of this discussion, it will prove necessary to refer to various additional transformation rules. These rules are not listed here in part because the present study is not of sufficient scope to allow for their precise formulation and in part because, in comparison with the rules just stated, the additional rules are not critically pertinent to the primary goal of this study: to establish a general framework for describing predicate complementation in English.

Notes

1. Noam Chomsky, Aspects of the Theory of Syntax (Cambridge, Mass.: The M.I.T. Press, 1965).

2. In the discussion to follow, the constituent AUX will be excluded from consideration. Although the behavior of the auxiliary, including at least Tense and Modal, is a pertinent dimension of the predicate complement system, the details of this behavior and its description go beyond the range of this study. It is unlikely, however, that a deeper study of the auxiliary in predicate complement constructions will result in a significant alteration of the general outlines of the predicate complement system as developed in this study.

3. When a constituent A is erased by a constituent B, A $\longrightarrow \emptyset$ only if A and B meet the conditions stipulated by the erasure principle.

4. For discussion of the auxiliary transformation, see Noam Chomsky, Syntactic Structures (The Hague: Mouton & Co., 1957).

2. A Defense of the Phrase Structure Rules

In the previous chapter, two phrase structure rules were shown to enumerate a variety of underlying phrase structures containing the constituent S. These rules constitute an assertion that either NP or VP may optionally dominate S in the underlying phrase structure representation for an infinite set of derivations. Underlying the formulation of these rules are the belief that the laws or rules governing allowable sequences of words in any natural language can be given in a simple manner and the empirical hypothesis that the simplest formulation of the rules best characterizes the varied instances of human linguistic competence. The purpose of this chapter is to show that diminished simplicity accompanies analyses of predicate complementation which do not postulate the recursion of S under the immediate domination of both NP and VP.

2.1 Noun Phrase Complementation

Consider the following pair of sentences which are traditionally described as active (1a) and passive (1b).

(1) a. the little boy took the book

b. the book was taken by the little boy

There is hardly a simpler formulation of the passive transformation than that according to which the noun phrases preceding and following the main verb of a sentence are inverted with a concurrent insertion of the passive morphemes be + en and by. Any speaker of English will attest that it is just this transformational process (in the literal sense) which relates sentences (1a) and (1b). Chomsky has shown, furthermore, that a passive transformation of this general form follows as a logical consequence from a general theory of language seeking to explain the linguistic abilities possessed by normal speakers of a language in some systematic fashion.[1]

But the generality of the passive transformation in its usual formulation, roughly the formulation given in Chapter 1, is at least superficially questionable with respect to certain observed phenomena of which sentences (2a) and (2b) are instances.

(2)   a.   Columbus demonstrated that the world is not flat

     b.   that the world is not flat was demonstrated by Columbus

It is as easy to believe that the phrase "that the world is not flat" is an instance of the constituent S as it is to believe that it is an instance of the constituent NP. For instance, phrases of this sort contain the constituent structure common to other instances of S. Under the appropriate conditions, such phrases can be passivized; for instance, I think that John hit the ball ⟶ I think that the ball was hit by John. It simply seems good sense to assert that any linguistic description which does not postulate that this phrase is an instance of S at some level of derivation could not achieve empirical adequacy. But it is not a priori obvious that successful linguistic descriptions must identify this phrase as an NP at some level of derivation.

Let us look more carefully at the passive transformation in terms of the most conservative analysis of the phrase "that the world is not flat," where this phrase is analyzed solely as an instance of S. Applying the same considerations that led us to relate (1a) and (1b), one observes that a new formulation of the passive transformation is required according to which a noun phrase preceding a verb and a sentence following the verb are inverted. The pair of sentences in (3) suggests an additional modification by which a sentence preceding a verb and a noun phrase following the verb are inverted.[2]

(3)   a.   that the doctor came at all surprised me

     b.   I was surprised that the doctor came at all

On the assumption that the phrases presented in these examples are instances of S, one is forced to a more elaborate formulation of the passive transformation, (4), in which sentences, in addition to noun phrases, can be inverted.

(4)   X $\begin{Bmatrix} NP \\ S \end{Bmatrix}$ AUX   V   (PREP) $\begin{Bmatrix} NP \\ S \end{Bmatrix}$ by + P   Y

    1   2   3   4   5   6   7   8   9 ⟹

    1, 6, 3, be + en, 4, 5, ∅, 7, 2, 9

The diminished generality of the passive transformation results not from the fact that phrases like "that the world is flat" must be analyzed as instances of S but from the assumption that such phrases are not also instances of NP. For if these phrases are assumed to be dominated by

NP in the structures underlying (2) and (3), then the original, more general formulation of the passive transformation is seen to be entirely adequate. If S as well as N can be dominated by NP (the formulation given by PS Rule 2 in Chapter 1), the original passive transformation will effectively generate the sentences in (1), (2), and (3). This is a consequence of the generalization that both N and S may be instances of NP.

The simpler statement of the passive transformation, made possible by the assumption that NP may dominate S, receives powerful support from the fact that the contrary assumption is simply not confirmed by observation. For instance, English contains a great many sentences such as (5), in which infinitival constructions, which must be analyzed as instances of S at some level, never undergo passivization.

(5)   a.   1.   I tended to think slowly
           2.   *to think slowly was tended by me

      b.   1.   John needs to go home early
           2.   *to go home early is needed by John

      c.   1.   she began to cry
           2.   *to cry was begun by her

Observations of this sort indicate that persistence in the assumption that S cannot be dominated by NP obliges us to propose further modifications in addition to a more complex statement of the passive transformation. In particular, it becomes necessary to include in the description a variety of apparently unsystematic restrictions on the application of the transformation in (4) so as to prevent the occurrence of sentences (5a. 2, b. 2, c. 2). If, on the other hand, NP can dominate S, then we can view the sentences in (5) as constructions that are instances of something other than noun phrase complementation, that is, as constructions whose underlying structures are quite distinct from those in (2) and (3). If NP dominates S in (2) and (3) but not in (5), then the sentences (5a. 2, b. 2, c. 2) are automatically ungrammatical since the passive transformation in its most general form applies only to NP's (dominating either N or S) and not to an S that is not dominated by NP.

The assumption that an NP can dominate S is instrumental in explaining a great many observed regularities in complement constructions that are superficially unrelated, that is, unrelated on the basis of simple inspection. The fact that the contrary assumption, just discarded for independent reasons, does not lead to an account of these regularities provides further support for the hypothesis proposed here. Consider the following pairs of sentences:

(6)   a.   1.   Columbus demonstrated that the world is not flat
           2.   that the world is not flat was demonstrated by Columbus
           3.   it was demonstrated by Columbus that the world is not flat

      b.   1.   that the doctor came at all surprises me
           2.   it surprises me that the doctor came at all

For much the same reason that led us to relate the sentences in (2), or the sentences in (3) for that matter, to a common underlying form, it is also necessary to relate sentence (6a. 1) to (6a. 2, 3) and the sentence (6b. 1) to (6b. 2). Careful observation of these examples indicates that any phrase (e.g., "that the doctor came at all") appearing before a verb phrase such as "surprised me" can also follow it. To assume that the two sentences are not derived from a common source is to diminish simplicity greatly. We shall return shortly to a proposal for capturing this generalization.

A reconsideration of PS Rule 2, as given in Chapter 1, reveals that the expansion of NP into the constitutents DET and N is obligatory. The expansion into DET N S is optional. If the foregoing considerations are correct, if the phrase "that the doctor came at all" is an S dominated immediately by NP, then one may question the formulation of PS Rule 2 since no N is observed preceding the phrase in (6b. 1). One might consider taking this fact as evidence that the expansion of NP into DET N is optional also. There is one general fact, however, which advises us that such a conclusion is in error. The sentences in (6) show that the pronoun "it" may appear in sentence initial position just in case the "that" phrase appears at the end of the sentence. Furthermore, the pronoun may not appear when the "that" phrase is in sentence initial position, as sentence (7) indicates.

(7)   *it that the doctor came at all surprised me

These facts suggest that it is the pronoun which determines the application of a transformational rule moving the "that" clause to the end of the sentence. Thus the structure underlying the sentences in (6b) might be formalized in terms of the phrase structure representation (8).[3]

(8)

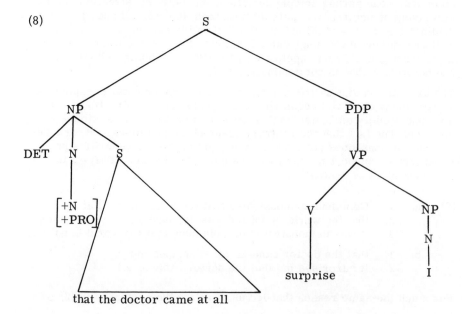

that the doctor came at all

The phrase structure configuration in (8) asserts that NP has been expanded into an N which carries the pronominal feature [+PRO] and a complement sentence S. We postulate that the sentences (6b. 1) and (6b. 2) are derived through the application of one of two extremely general rules defined upon this configuration. The first of these rules is the extraposition transformation, defined in Chapter 1, according to which an S following a pronoun is extraposed to the end of the string, thereby yielding (6b. 2). A second transformation, the pronoun deletion transformation,[4] defined in Chapter 1, deletes the pronoun when it occurs immediately before S, thus producing sentence (6b. 1). It is clear that the sentences in (6a) can be similarly derived.[5]

Further support for PS Rule 2 is provided by the fact that both of the transformations just discussed, T_E and T_{PD}, which are required to explain the relatedness of (6b. 1) and (6b. 2), are independently motivated in other instances. Consider, for example, the following pair of sentences.

(9)   a.   I would like for you to be there very much

       b.   I would like very much for you to be there

On the assumption that the phrase "for you to be there" is an instance of noun phrase complementation described by PS Rule 2, the relation of (9a) to (9b) becomes an automatic consequence of T_E, according to which the phrase is extraposed to the end of the string.

The conclusion that PS Rule 2 is valid is supported by yet another consideration, specifically, the limitations on the occurrence of "pseudocleft" sentences. The problem posed by these sentences is that they are not predictable simply from the inspection of noncleft sentences. Consider the differences between the following pairs of sentences:

(10)   a.   1.   I hate you to do things like that
             2.   what I hate is for you to do things like that

       b.   1.   we prefer you to stay right here
             2.   what we prefer is for you to stay right here

       c.   1.   I defy you to do things like that
             2.   *what I defy is for you to do things like that

       d.   1.   we tempted you to stay right here
             2.   *what we tempted was for you to stay right here

Eschewing the details of wh attachment and pseudocleft sentence derivation, we may nonetheless suppose that the derivation of these sentences depends upon a noun phrase complement structure. If this conjecture is correct, then the grammaticality of (10a. 2, b. 2) implies that the sentences (10a. 1, b. 1) have noun phrase complementation, where the phrases "you to do things like that" and "you to stay right here" are what remains of an underlying structure in which these phrases were generated as S's under the domination of NP. Independent proof of this claim stems from the possible extraposition of these phrases as in (11).

(11) a.   I hate very much for you to do things like that

b.   I prefer very much for you to stay right here

Since the sentences (10c. 2, d. 2) are ungrammatical, our hypothesis leads us to the conclusion that the sentences (10c. 1, d. 1) are not instances of noun phrase complementation, a prediction sustained by the fact that extraposition is impossible for these sentences.[6]

(12) a.   *I defy very much for you to do things like that

b.   *we tempted very much for you to stay right here

If the hypothesis is true that the pseudocleft sentences just discussed depend upon the application of PS Rule 2, producing noun phrase complements, the grammar predicts a successful derivation of the pseudocleft sentence for those constructions, mentioned earlier, where the noun phrase complement analysis was proposed. The fact that the following derivatives of the sentences in (6) are grammatical confirms this prediction.

(13) a.   what Columbus demonstrated was that the world is not flat

b.   what was demonstrated by Columbus was that the world is not flat

(14) a.   what surprised me was that the doctor came at all

b.   what I was surprised at was that the doctor came at all

2. 2   Verb Phrase Complementation

Our acceptance of PS Rule 1, which variously expands VP into S, requires, first, a demonstration that PS Rule 2 is inappropriate for certain constructions and, second, a valid argument that PS Rule 1 is the most general formulation accounting for the residue of cases not handled by PS Rule 2. Toward these ends, consider the following data:

(15) a.   1.   everyone preferred to remain silent
      2.   to remain silent was preferred by everyone
      3.   what everyone preferred was to remain silent

b.   1.   John tended to play with his little brother often
      2.   *to play with his little brother often was tended by John
      3.   *what John tended was to play with his little brother often

The paradigm (15a) exhibits the properties that are generally associated with noun phrase complementation: passivization of the entire complement sentence (in this case, "to remain silent") and the presence of a pseudocleft sentence. These properties are not, however, observed in the second paradigm (15b).

The current formulation of transformational theory allows at least two devices that are sufficiently powerful to prevent the generation of the ungrammatical sentences in (15b). The first alternative postulates that (15a) and (15b) have similar underlying structures but differ in the specification of the transformational rules applying to this structure. In other words, the verb "tend" is marked in such a way that both the passive transformation and those transformations instrumental in the derivation of the pseudocleft sentence are not applicable. The second alternative claims that (15b) is not an instance of noun phrase complementation but rather a paradigm whose underlying form is something like (1) in Chapter 1. In the second analysis, the verb "tend" is also marked, but not for the application of transformations. Rather, the verb has a strict subcategorization marker[7] which permits its occurrence before the constituent S. In this description, the ungrammaticality of (15b. 2) and (15b. 3) follows from the fact that neither the passive transformation nor the pseudocleft sentence transformations apply to an S that is not immediately dominated by NP.

Of the two alternatives, the second, which assumes (15a) and (15b) to have different underlying structures, seems to be more general. In either analysis, a strict subcategorization marker on the verb is required. In the first analysis, this marker stipulates that the verb "tend" must occur immediately preceding an NP that must itself dominate S. In the second analysis, the strict subcategorization marker simply requires that the verb "tend" occur immediately preceding the constituent S. Thus, just one example of unnecessary complexity in the first analysis is the specification that the NP following the verb must dominate S. This requirement follows from the fact that the verb "tend" is otherwise intransitive.[8] Since the second analysis asserts that the verb may occur only before S, the ungrammaticality of (16) is an automatic consequence and requires no additional feature specification.

(16) a. *I tended the ball

   b. *I tended something

Even if the two analyses were equally simple with respect to strict subcategorization markers, we should prefer the second analysis over the first on yet another ground. In the first analysis, where it is assumed that the verb "tend" occurs immediately preceding an NP, it becomes necessary to specify a set of transformations for the construction. In particular, such a verb must be marked for the nonapplication of the passive transformation and the pseudocleft sentence transformations. This is a relatively simple task. However, the crucial point is that in the second analysis, which assumes that "tend" is followed by S in the underlying structure, such a feature specification is totally unnecessary, since the transformations under discussion do not apply to an S that is not dominated immediately by the constituent NP. Thus the first analysis, treating (15b) as an instance of noun phrase complementation, fails on two counts. First, this analysis requires an unnecessarily complex strict subcategorization statement. Second, it requires a fairly elaborate set of restrictions on allowable transformations, which is totally unnecessary if it is hypothesized that (15b) is not an instance of noun phrase complementation.

It is thus a necessary conclusion that there are a number of complement constructions that cannot be instances of noun phrase complementation. That these constructions are most fruitfully analyzed as instances of verb phrase complementation follows from various considerations on the operation of the identity erasure transformation T_{EI} as given in Chapter 1. In the noun phrase complement system, the deletion of the subject of the complement sentence is often obligatory when it is identical to the subject of the main or including sentence. Consider the following cases:

(17) a. I love Bill to play the piano

     b. I love to play the piano

     c. *I love me to play the piano

On the basis of this evidence alone, the simplest formulation of the identity erasure transformation would stipulate that the subject of the complement sentence is obligatorily deleted just in case it is identical to the first noun phrase to the left of the complement sentence in the main sentence. This statement is consistent not only for many instances of noun phrase complementation but also for all instances of the type of complementation exemplified by (15b. 1). Furthermore, this formulation holds for transitive verbs[9] which take the type of complement found in the same example, as is illustrated in the following instances.

(18) a. they tempted John to leave early

     b. we forced John to ignore his work

This formulation collapses in the face of certain adverbial constructions representing a degenerate form of the prepositional locution "in order to."

(19) a. I sold the boat (in order) to save money

     b. she took the car (in order) to buy bread

In these cases, the implicit subject of the adverbial sentence is not the first noun phrase to the left in each case; rather it is the second noun phrase to the left. The problem gets even more complex when we observe instances where identity to the right is apparently required. Consider, for instance, the following sentences:

(20) a. can you expect it of him to do what is right always

     b. I absolutely require it of you to be here on time

One will readily appreciate that the phrases "it to do what is right" and "it to be here on time" are noun phrase complements and that the sentences in (20) assume their form by virtue of the application of the extraposition transformation. The noun phrase to which the subject of the

complement sentence must be identical lies to the right of the complement sentence, thus irreparably damaging the left-identity hypothesis.

All of these difficulties may be resolved by the adoption of an extremely
general principle governing the application of the transformation that
deletes the subject of complement constructions. This principle becomes
immediately apparent in diagrams (21), (22), and (23) upon examination
of the phrase structures underlying (17), (19), and (20).

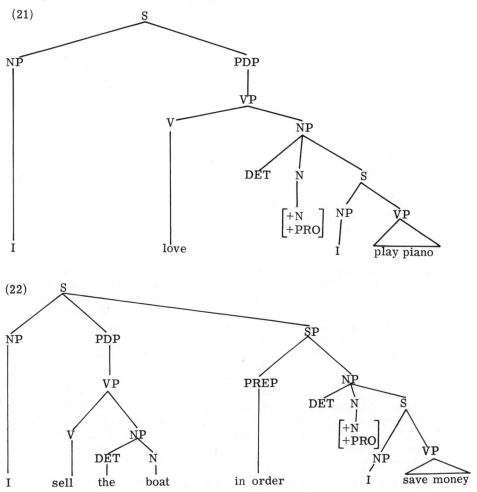

The three phrase structures depicted in diagrams (21)-(23) suggest that
an NP_j can be erased by the identity erasure transformation just in case
there is some sentence S_α (a complement sentence) such that (1) NP_j is
dominated by S_α; (2) NP_i neither dominates nor is dominated by S_α; and
(3) for any NP_k which neither dominates nor is dominated by S_α, the distance between NP_j and NP_k is greater than the distance between NP_j and
NP_i (where the distance between two nodes is defined in terms of the
number of branches in the path connecting them). In diagrams (21) and

(23)

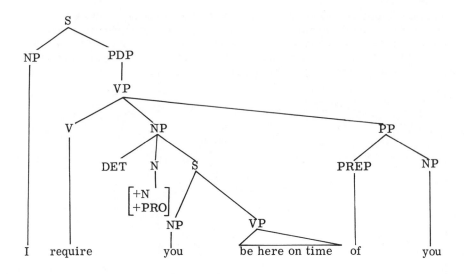

(22), the "erasing" NP's are the subject NP's of the main sentence. In (23), the erasing NP is the NP "you" in the prepositional phrase of the main sentence. In all three phrase structures, the erased NP happens to be the underlying subject of the complement sentence. The identity erasure transformation asserts only that the erased NP must be the one that follows the complementizing morphemes "for" and "POSS." This correctly allows both the identity erasure transformation and the erasure principle that governs its application to range over derived subjects, as in cases where the passive transformation has applied to the complement sentence. As will be seen in the discussion to follow, the erasure principle accounts for most cases of identity erasure in English and has few exceptions. The fact that the erasure principle applies with such remarkable precision to so many cases suggests that the apparent exceptions may indeed be false counterexamples, a possibility which is attested by considerations to be raised later.

Returning to the question of whether the complement constructions in (18) and (15b) are instances of verb phrase complementation, we find that the erasure principle provides a ready answer. On the supposition that the complement sentences in (18) lie outside the verb phrase but under the domination of predicate phrase PDP,[10] the erasure principle breaks down. This follows from the fact that, if the complement is not dominated by the verb phrase, then the subject NP of the complement sentence is ambiguously connected to the main sentence. This is readily seen in the hypothetical phrase structure (24), where the subject NP of the complement sentence is equidistant from the subject and object of the main sentence.

(24)

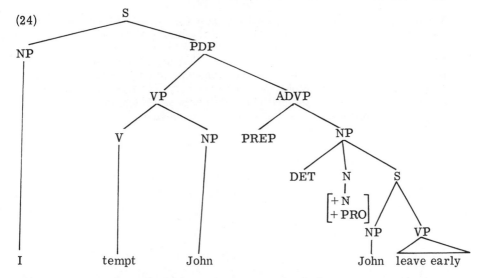

The situation becomes worse for sentences like (25) which have the underlying structure (26).

(25)   I prevail upon John to go

(26)

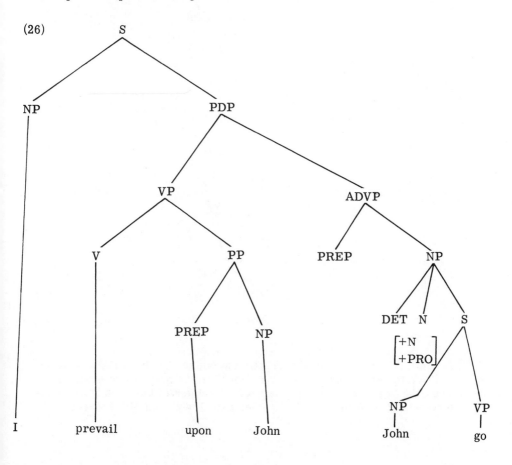

The erasure principle cannot apply in the case of (26). Furthermore, if the subject of "to go" had been "I," the grammar would make the false prediction that the implicit subject of "to go" in (25) is "I" rather than "John." If, on the other hand, we postulate that the complement sentence is a verb phrase complement, derived through the application of PS Rule 1, then the erasure principle operates correctly. This is observed in diagram (27a, b) where the structures underlying (18a) and (25) are assumed to exemplify verb phrase complementation.

(27a)

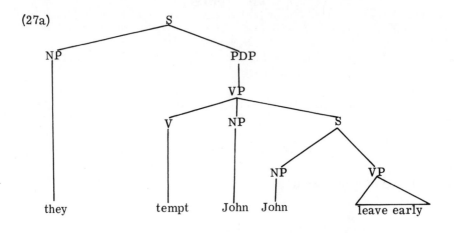

(27b)

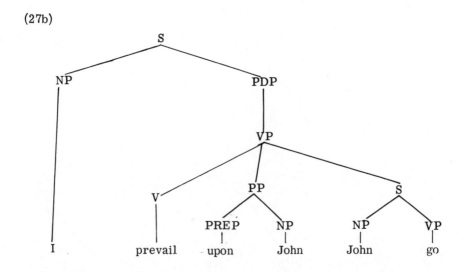

In (27a), the erasing NP is correctly the object NP of the main sentence. In (27b), the erasing NP is the NP "John" in the prepositional phrase. Thus, the grammar predicts the implicit subject of the complement sentences in (27a, b) to be "John" rather than "they" and "I," respectively.

Not positing the complement sentences "to leave early" and "to go" as instances of verb phrase complementation in (27) destroys one's ability to generalize the identity erasure transformation. Without assuming verb phrase complementation, the principle governing identity erasure would, in any case, become so complex as to be unserviceable. Since the analysis of verb phrase complementation is a consequence of the most general formulation of erasure principle, the necessity of adopting such a construct as the verb phrase complement seems unavoidable.

The two types of complementation under discussion in this chapter by no means exhaust the complementation systems of English. Other kinds of sentential embedding are quite common. Among these are relativization, as exemplified by (28), and subordination of various types (29).

(28)   the man who arrived yesterday left today

(29)   a.   she laughed because the joke was funny

      b.   being late to dinner, I got nothing to eat.

While it is not at all certain that the complementation represented by (28) and (29) shares no common properties with noun phrase and verb phrase complementation as defined by phrase structure Rules 1 and 2, it is nonetheless clear that noun phrase and verb phrase complementation presupposes a fairly intricate set of rules that seem at present to play but a small role in other complement systems. The remainder of the present work will be devoted to the rules required to handle noun phrase and verb phrase complementation (henceforth collectively referred to as predicate complementation) and their implementation in the grammar.

Notes

1.   Cf. Noam Chomsky, Syntactic Structures (The Hague: Mouton & Co., 1957), especially Chapter 7; for further discussion of the passive transformation, see R. B. Lees, The Grammar of English Nominalizations (The Hague: Mouton & Co., 1960); J. J. Katz and P. M. Postal, An Integrated Theory of Linguistic Descriptions (Cambridge, Mass.: The M.I.T. Press, 1964); Chomsky, Aspects of the Theory of Syntax (Cambridge, Mass.: The M.I.T. Press, 1965).

2.   The derivation of the sentence (3b) requires essentially two steps. The application of the passive transformation to the structure underlying (3b) will yield the string "I be+en surprise by that the doctor came at all." The agentive preposition "by" is subsequently deleted by the application of a general preposition deletion transformation discussed in Chapter 4.

3.   The constituent PDP is expanded into VP and an optional adverbial which usually takes the form of a prepositional phrase, as in time and place adverbials, e.g., "at dawn" or "in the woods." Since the present study does not deal with these adverbials, the constituent PDP will, for the most part, dominate VP directly.

4. The present study assumes that the pronoun "it" in sentences like (6a. 3) and (6b. 2) is introduced into the underlying structure by the same rules that introduce lexical items into the underlying structure. The grammar thus requires a transformational rule deleting this pronoun in the appropriate environments. Since no transformational rules are formulated in terms of the phonological matrix of this pronoun, it is entirely conceivable that the phonological matrix for the pronoun is introduced by ordered "spelling" rules perhaps of the following form which apply after the transformational rules.

a. $$\begin{bmatrix} +N \\ +PRO \end{bmatrix} \longrightarrow \quad \text{it/} \begin{bmatrix} \begin{bmatrix} \underline{\quad} \end{bmatrix}_N \end{bmatrix}_{NP}$$

b. $\quad$ it $\longrightarrow \emptyset$ / ____ ADV (optional)

5. The derivation of sentence (6a. 1) does not presuppose the application of the passive transformation, whereas this transformation is requisite to the derivation of sentences (6a. 2, 3).

6. It is reasonable to argue that the sentences in (12) are blocked by virtue of the fact that the adverbial "very much" is inappropriate for verbs like "defy" and "tempt" in certain dialects of English. In such dialects, sentences like the following are ungrammatical:

*I defy you to do things like that very much
*we tempted you to stay right here very much

But this counterargument collapses when suitable adverbials are employed, as is seen in the following pairs:

I defied him to buy a house consistently
*I defied consistently for him to buy a house

we tempted him to stay home cleverly
*we tempted cleverly for him to stay home

7. Cf. Chomsky, <u>Aspects of the Theory of Syntax</u>, for a discussion of subcategorization.

8. The intransitive verb "tend" must, of course, be distinguished from the transitive homonymous verb "tend," as in "the shepherd tended the flock." It is the former which is ungrammatical in the sentences in (16).

9. The assumption that the verbs in (18) are transitive follows from two considerations, one of which has not yet been discussed. First, the phrases "John to leave early" and "John to ignore his work" are not instances of noun phrase complementation. If they were, we should expect sentences like *"what they tempted was for John to leave early" and *"what we forced was for John to ignore his work" to be grammatical. Second, identity erasure is obligatory for all

instances of verb phrase complementation. Thus the grammaticality of the sentences in (18) implies that "John" in both of these sentences originates as an object noun phrase.

10. The assumption that complement sentences like "to leave early" in (24) are under the domination of the PDP is, of course, more conservative than the assumption that this sentence is under the domination of SP, the subordinate adverbial phrase, which is immediately dominated by S. Since the erasure principle fails, however, even for the most conservative assumption, there is little reason to investigate other possible analyses for the sentences in (18).

3. Complementizing Morphemes and Their Introduction into the Underlying Structure

One of the properties of predicate complements that distinguishes them from other types of complements is a unique set of markers taking the form of single and paired morphemes. Such markers, including the morphemes that, for, to, POSS, ing, and others,[1] will be referred to as complementizing morphemes or simply complementizers. This study will deal with these five complementizers:

(1)   I think that Fords are too expensive

(2)   I dislike arguing about silly matters

(3)   I am concerned about John's being so lazy

(4)   the king ordered the proclamation to be read

(5)   I should like very much for you to reconsider your refusal

Certain mutual inclusions and exclusions in the set of complementizers exemplified in (1)–(5) are immediately apparent. The complementizer "for" co-occurs only with the complementizer "to." The complementizer "POSS" co-occurs only with "ing." The complementizer "that" occurs alone, never with either "ing" or "to." Sentences like the following are impossible in English:

(6)   *I anticipated John's to argue with me

(7)   *I can't stand for John being late to supper

(8)   a. *I think that John to be late

      b. *I think that John being late

It may thus prove convenient to speak of the "that" complementizer, the "for-to" complementizer, and the "POSS-ing" complementizer.

There are two in some sense distinct questions that one might raise concerning the complementizers. First, what are the considerations involved in determining the way in which the complementizers are introduced into various predicate complement constructions? Second, if we assume that the descriptive constructs devised with respect to the first question achieve a reasonable level of adequacy, what factors must be taken into consideration in describing the behavior of the complementizers after they have been introduced into the underlying structure of a predicate complement construction? The present study deals primarily with the second question, although, as will be seen in the following pages, it presupposes certain aspects of complementizer introduction that are still unproved.

Implicit in the term "complementizer" is the idea that these morphemes are a function of predicate complementation and not the property of any particular sentence or set of sentences. Thus there is no structure underlying any declarative sentence in English that cannot, in some other derivation, be the structure underlying a predicate complement sentence. This would seem to imply that the rule or set of rules employed in the introduction of a complementizer into a predicate complement construction must be either a context-sensitive rewriting rule or a rule with transformational power, since it is necessary to account for the observation that other types of complement sentences as well as main sentences (themselves not predicate complement sentences) do not contain complementizers of the type under discussion. For instance, strings like those in (6) are not sentences in English.

(6) a. *that John came early

b. *for John to have done it

c. *John's having done it

The fact that there is some evidence supporting the view that context-sensitive rewriting rules are unnecessary baggage in the syntactic component of the grammar does not, however, imply that complementizer introduction is to be a transformational process entirely. Viewing a transformational rule as a "filter,"[2] we find it entirely possible that the complementizers are derived in the underlying structure through the operation of context-free rewriting rules. The application of such rules would thus provide an object that a transformation can interpret and mark as either well formed or not well formed. The present formulation of the theory, therefore, allows either for the phrase structure introduction of the complementizers or for a completely transformational introduction. In the absence of compelling evidence for accepting one formulation over the other, and since it is probably true that the selection of either alternative will not affect the discussion of the operations defined over complementizers one way or the other, the clarity of the following exposition will profit by arbitrarily adopting the transformational alternative simply because this option is probably the most familiar. But it should be kept in mind that, although this option offers a description of complementizer introduction, there is as yet little evidence to suggest that it is the right one.

At least three considerations play a role in the introduction of complementizers into the underlying structure. The first concerns the classification of the complementizers and the notation in which this classification is framed. A cursory glance at the list of transformational rules in
Chapter 1 reveals that several transformations are sensitive either to a
"for-to" complementizer or to a "POSS-ing" complementizer. In most
cases, the "that" complementizer exemplifies properties markedly different from the remaining two complementizers. This generalization
can be captured if, in the grammar, it is more expensive, that is, less
simple, to refer to just the "for-to" complementizer or to just the
"POSS-ing" complementizer than it is to refer to both together. Toward
this end, we might propose a binary feature hierarchy for classifying the
complementizers where this hierarchy contains the following redundancy
rules:

(7) $[+C] \longrightarrow [\pm D]$

      $[+D] \longrightarrow [\pm E]$

      $\begin{bmatrix} +C \\ -D \end{bmatrix}$ is realized morphemically as "that"

      $\begin{bmatrix} +C \\ +D \\ -E \end{bmatrix}$ is realized morphemically as "for-to"

      $\begin{bmatrix} +C \\ +D \\ +E \end{bmatrix}$ is realized morphemically as "POSS-ing"

This notation provides precisely the correct generalization. Should a
rule in the grammar have to refer either to "for-to" or "POSS-ing"
separately, the structural description will have to list at least three
features, namely (8) or (9), for the "for-to" and "POSS-ing" complementizers respectively.

(8) $\begin{bmatrix} +C \\ +D \\ -E \end{bmatrix}$

(9) $\begin{bmatrix} +C \\ +D \\ +E \end{bmatrix}$

On the other hand, should it be necessary to refer to both complementizers together, the structural description needs to contain only two features (10), since it does not matter whether the feature "E" is marked
"+" or "−".

(10) $\begin{bmatrix} +C \\ +D \end{bmatrix}$

Furthermore, reference to all three complementizers requires only one feature [+C], since it does not matter here whether the feature "D" is "+" or "−".

On the additional assumption that the complementizing features comprise a feature system distinct from other features that might be postulated for lexical items, an assumption which will affect this presentation trivially even if it is false, it becomes possible to simplify further the representation of the complementizers.

(11) 1.   that, for-to, POSS-ing   [+C]

     2.   that   [−D]

     3.   for-to, POSS-ing   [+D]

Keeping this discussion in mind, we turn to the second issue that plays a role in the formulation of the transformational apparatus introducing complementizers into the underlying structure. This issue concerns the statement of the restrictions holding between the main sentence and the complementizer of the predicate complement sentence. Inspection of the following verb phrase complement data readily indicates that the choice of the complementizer in the verb phrase complement is dependent upon the verb in the main sentence.

(12) a.   they prevailed upon me to help out

     b.   *they prevailed upon me that I help out

     c.   *they prevailed upon me helping out

(13) a.   the noise forced me to stop working

     b.   *the noise forced me that I stop working

     c.   *the noise forced me stopping working

There are few, if any, apparent counterexamples to the empirical claim that the "that" complementizer never functions as the complementizer of a verb phrase complement.[3] The issue is not so clear cut with the "POSS-ing" complementizer. One observes, for instance, the following sentences:

(14) a.   we heard him running down the street

     b.   I imagined myself eating at the Ritz

It may be argued, perhaps, that what appears to be an instance of the "POSS-ing" complementizer in the complement constructions (14) is simply a degenerate form of the "for-to" complementizer where the "to" is deleted before the progressive morphemes "be-ing." In this view, the constructions in (15) are earlier stages in the derivation of (14).

(15) a.   *we heard him to be running down the street

     b.   I imagined myself to be eating at the Ritz

Although such an analysis appeals to the semantic intuition that the activities defined in the complement sentence are, in some sense, ongoing, the fact that the progressive morphemes do not occur freely in the complement sentence partially confirms the view that verb phrase complements may have "POSS-ing" as well as "for-to" complementizers. Consider the following sentences:

(16)   a.   I imagined myself owning a mansion

      b.   *I am owning a mansion

Since the verb "own" cannot take the progressive form in general, it is difficult to see how the phrase "owning a mansion" could be an instance of the progressive. The verb "own" is not, of course, restricted with respect to the "POSS-ing" complementizer, as we observe in the following noun phrase complement construction.

(17)   I dislike their owning such a big car

On the other hand, constructions such as (18) seem to require a description in which "ing" is, in Fillmore's sense, a <u>telescoped progressive</u>.[4]

(18)   a.   I felt the rope slip

      b.   I felt the rope slipping

Since the complementizers seem, in general, not to affect the semantic interpretation of the complement sentence, it becomes difficult to explain the difference in meanings between (18a) and (18b) on the assumption that the "ing" in (18b) is the complementizer "ing." But this difference would be accounted for if one assumed that "ing" in (18b) is the progressive "ing."[5]

The question of whether or not there are instances of the "POSS-ing" complementizer in verb phrase complement constructions is, in a certain sense, irrelevant to a successful demonstration that there are restrictions between the verb in the main sentence and the complementizer in the verb complement sentence since there is little question that the "that" complementizer is so restricted.[6] Should it turn out that the "POSS-ing" complementizer never occurs in verb complement constructions, this will mean simply that whatever mechanism prevents the generation of the complementizer "that" in such constructions will also prohibit the generation of "POSS-ing." In the present discussion, it will be assumed that the "POSS-ing" complementizer does, in fact, appear in verb phrase complement constructions since this complementizer seems to be necessary for intransitive verb phrase complement constructions.

To say that the selection of either the "for-to" or the "POSS-ing" complementizer in a verb phrase complement construction depends upon the verb in the main sentence implies a descriptive apparatus which posits that verbs are marked with particular complementizer features in the lexicon that may appear in their verb phrase complements. We propose, in other words, that verbs contain features indicating which complementizer is possible in a coordinate verb phrase complement. In terms of the notation suggested earlier, this means that a verb may be marked with the features [+D] [+E] if the verb has a "POSS-ing" complementizer, with the features [+D] [−E] if the verb has a "for-to" complementizer, and with the feature [+D] in the event that the verb takes either the "POSS-ing" or the "for-to" complementizer. Furthermore, should a verb be found that takes all three complementizers, an apparently unlikely event in a verb phrase complement construction, this will be marked simply [+C].

The complementizer placement transformation, case C, precludes the possibility of the complementizer "that" being generated in a verb phrase complement by stipulating that all verbs which take verb phrase complement constructions be marked at least [+D]. The variable "α," ranging over the feature coefficients, is introduced into the transformation in order to ensure that the coefficient of the feature "E" in the verb is identical to the coefficient of the introduced complementizers. Case C of this transformation states, for instance, that if the verb in the main sentence is marked with the features [+D] [−E], then the features [+D] [−E] are first introduced into the verb phrase complement sentence immediately preceding an initial noun phrase under the domination of S. Case D of this transformation asserts that those features introduced by cases B and C preceding the initial noun phrase of the complement sentence are duplicated immediately preceding V, have, or be under the domination of VP. Subsequently, these feature clusters are realized morphophonemically as "to" before V, have, or be and as "for" elsewhere, or as "ing" before V, have, or be and as "POSS" elsewhere.

Turning to noun phrase complementation, ones notices that complementizer selection is somewhat broader in the sense that although the complementizer "that" is a possibility, there are restrictions nonetheless. Consider the following sentences:

(19) a. I think that John will be late

     b. *I think John's being late

(20) a. I want you to hurry home

     b. *I want that you hurry home

(21) a. I relish owning catamarans

     b. *I relish that I own catamarans

On the surface, there seems little doubt that the restrictions upon complementizer selection in noun phrase complement constructions can be handled in a fashion similar to verb phrase complementizer restrictions. The question arises of whether it is the noun in the noun phrase containing the noun phrase complement (henceforth the head of the noun phrase complement construction) that specifies the restrictions or, once again, the verb in the main sentence. The latter alternative has a certain appeal stemming from the fact that if the former alternative is taken, it will still be necessary to mark the verb with the same information for purposes of strict subclassification. In other words, even if a particular complementizer is determined by the head of the noun phrase complement construction, verbs must be marked according to their capacity to appear either before or after such a complement construction. Thus the maximum generality would appear to be preserved if the restrictions are marked on the verb.

Despite its superficial desirability, the specification of noun phrase complementizer restrictions in the verb of the main sentence proves to be inadequate on the basis of considerations to be examined in some detail later. Briefly, the objection is as follows: It is necessary to postulate complementizer features on pronoun heads of noun phrase complement constructions since the simplest possible formulation of the preposition deletion transformation is defined over a pronoun marked either with the feature $[-D]$ or with the feature $[-E]$. If this hypothesis is valid, then the supposition that the verb determines the restrictions on noun phrase complementizers becomes improbable since it allows for the generation of ungrammatical strings. Imagine the following situation: A "that" complementizer is selected for the noun phrase complement in some prepositional phrase within the verb phrase on the basis of the feature $[-D]$ in the verb of the main sentence. At the same time, a pronoun in the noun phrase complement construction is generated with the features $[+D][+E]$. The grammar will subsequently produce a sentence containing a noun phrase complement with a "that" complementizer before which the introduced preposition will not have been deleted, as in (22).

(22) *I decided on that John will represent us.

The resulting ungrammatical sentence is a function of the fact that there is no dependency established between the complementizing features on the verb and those on the pronoun. The most readily apparent solution is to make use of the strict categorization mechanism to insure that verbs and the relevant constituents are marked for the same set of features. But once this is accomplished, the original feature specification, designed for the verbal determination of complementizer restrictions in noun phrase complements, becomes redundant since the features on the pronominal head of the noun phrase complement construction may be employed in the same capacity. Thus the greatest generality is achieved if we postulate that the head of the noun phrase complement is the constituent that specifies those features which determine the noun phrase complements. For these reasons, the complementizer placement transformation in Chapter 1 has two cases, a noun case and a verb case. In the final analysis, there is probably an adjective case as well, but this topic will be the focus of much later discussion in Chapter 6.

A final case that must be resolved by any successful complementizer introduction device occurs when, under certain conditions, complementizers preclude the occurrence of tense and modals. More specifically, modals cannot occur in predicate complement constructions containing either the "for-to" complementizer or the "POSS-ing" complementizer. For instance, sentences like the following are ungrammatical:

(23) a. *I asked John to will hit the ball

   b. John will hit the ball

(24) a. *I dislike John's can playing the piano

   b. John can play the piano

On the other hand, there appears to be no comparable modal restriction on predicate complement sentences containing the "that" complementizer, a claim supported by the following data:

(25) a. I think that John will hit the ball

   b. I suppose that John can play the piano

The modal restriction can be incorporated into the complementizer placement transformation fairly easily, but the solution provided by the complementizer placement transformation in Chapter 1 has its limitations and must be considered to have at best a rough correspondence to the facts. What is not explained by the formulation of the complementizer placement transformation postulated for the present work is the fact that quite often a particular modal interpretation is implicit in a complement construction containing either the "for-to" or "POSS-ing" complementizer. Consider the following sentences:

(26) a. I expect that John will go

   b. I expect John to go

(27) a. I anticipate that John will not want to leave

   b. I anticipate John's not wanting to leave

(28) is it possible for John to leave early

The modal "will" is, in some sense at least, an implicit aspect of the interpretation of the complement sentences in (26b) and (27b). Similarly, the modal "can" (on one of its readings at least) is an aspect of the interpretation of the complement sentence in (28). On the other hand, in the great majority of the predicate complement constructions there is no obvious modal interpretation whatever. These hazy facts suggest that a certain difficulty may await the apparatus formulated to account for the gross modal exclusion with the "for-to" and "POSS-ing" complementizers. Since all syntactic and lexical material necessary for the semantic interpretation of a sentence is included in the underlying structure, we are forced to believe that the modal interpretation of (26b, 27b, 28) results from either the actual existence of the modal in the underlying structure of the predicate complement sentence or, more likely, from some special, idiosyncratic feature of particular verbs for which modal interpretation is necessary. There is, as yet, little evidence on which to base an evaluation of the two alternatives. But, in the event that the first alternative is favored, it will, of course, be necessary to revise the complementizer placement transformation significantly. Perhaps this fact itself is a hint that the second alternative will turn out to be correct.

Notes

1. A second major class of complementizers with which this study does not deal includes the wh complementizer as in the following cases:
   a. I dislike it when you do that
   b. I often wonder (about) why he does these things
   c. I know where he went
   d. everyone understands how he does it
   e. what ne is doing is useless

   Also functioning as complementizing morphemes are if and whether, as in the following sentences:
   a. I doubt if he is going
   b. I wonder whether he is going

2. Noam Chomsky, Aspects of the Theory of Syntax (Cambridge, Mass.: The M.I.T. Press, 1965).

3. A possible counterexample is the following sentence with the verb "pretend":

   I pretended that I was a pilot

   The fact that the "that" clause neither passivizes nor participates in the pseudocleft sentence with the verb "pretend" suggests that this phrase may be a verb phrase complement.

   *that I was a pilot was pretended by me
   *what I pretended was that I was a pilot

   These data are hardly reliable, however, since there are dialects of English which apparently accept the pseudocleft sentence.

4. C. J. Fillmore, "The Position of Embedding Transformations in a Grammar," Word, 19, (1963), 208-231.

5. This observation was suggested to the author by Edward S. Klima.

6. It should be pointed out in this respect that there is reason to believe that sentence (14b) is not an instance of verb phrase complementation in the first place. These considerations are raised in Chapter 4. It may thus be the case that transitive verb phrase complementation allows only the "for-to" complementizer.

4. Noun Phrase Complementation

The discussion in Chapters 2 and 3 showed, first, that an adequate linguistic description of English syntax must posit noun phrase complement
structures having the properties characterized by phrase structure
Rule 2 and, second, that such complement constructions are marked by
complementizing morphemes whose privileges of occurrence are specified by the complementizer placement transformation T_{CP}.

The present chapter deals with three distinct instances of noun phrase
complementation. We shall be concerned with two instances of this construct which are characterized by phrase structure Rule 1, where either
the object of the main verb or the noun phrase in the prepositional
phrase following the main verb may dominate a noun phrase complement
construction. Furthermore, we shall also study the instance of noun
phrase complementation when the dominating noun phrase is the underlying subject of a sentence, a construction produced by the rewriting rule
which yields NP, AUX, VP on the basis of the symbol S. Since the transformational rules governing these cases are, in part, dependent upon
complementizer selection (the properties of the various complementizers
being in some ways distinct in noun phrase complement constructions),
this investigation ranges actually over nine cases and not over three.

4.1 Object Complementation

The term "object complementation" is a mnemonic making reference to
the instance of noun phrase complementation that arises through the
expansion of VP into at least V, NP. The application of phrase structure
Rule 2 subsequently yields the string V, DET, N, S. And it is to this particular configuration that attention is directed in the discussion of the
properties of object complementation.

4.1.1. The "that" complementizer

It was mentioned in an earlier discussion that noun phrase complements may contain one of three complementizers depending upon the particular verb in the main sentence. In this section, we shall study the transformational rules required in the event that the complementizer determined by the main verb is the complementizer "that." Toward this end, consider the following paradigm:[1]

(1) a.   they doubt it that you will do

     b.   they doubt that you will go

     c.   they doubt you will go

     d.   they doubt it very much that you will go

     e.   they doubt very much that you will go

     f.   that you will go is doubted by them

     g.   it is doubted by them that you will go

In terms of phrase structure Rules 1 and 2, the structure shared by all of the sentences in (1) is specified in diagram (2).

(2)

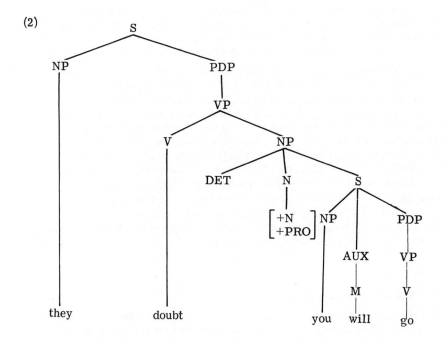

The relatedness of (1f) and (1g) is partially reflected, therefore, in the fact that both sentences have a common underlying source, shown in diagram (2). But this fact in itself does not tell us very much about the derivation of (1f) and (1g) since there are at least two analyses based upon the common underlying structure that, at least superficially, yield equally simple derivations of the two sentences. To settle this issue, it is necessary to take into consideration other factors besides the common underlying structure. In the first analysis, the two sentences share only the underlying structure. In the second analysis, the two sentences share not only the underlying structure but also an intermediate stage of the derivation in the sense that both sentences are the result of certain transformations applying to a string that is itself the product of a transformational rule applied to the underlying structure. Since so much ultimately depends upon the decision made here, it will be fruitful to study these alternatives in greater detail.

Both analyses presuppose the application of the passive transformation Tp as formulated in Chapter 1. But here the similarity ends. In the first analysis, sentence (1f) results from having deleted the pronominal head of the complement construction prior to the application of the passive transformation. The passive transformation thus applies to a string of roughly the following structure:

(3)   they doubt [[that you will go]   ]
                                       S NP

Since the passive transformation applies to any constituent NP such that this constituent conforms to the structural description specified in Chapter 1, it follows that this transformation will apply to (3), producing the string ultimately realized as sentence (1f). In the same analysis, sentence (1g) results from not having deleted the pronominal head prior to the application of the passive transformation. According to this consideration, the passive transformation applies to a string (4a), thus producing the string (4b).

(4)   a.   they doubt [[it] [that you will go]   ]
                          N   S NP

       b.   [[it] [that you will go]   ] is doubted by them
               N   S NP

Subsequently, the extraposition transformation, T_E, as defined in Chapter 1, applies to the string (4b), separating the noun phrase complement from the pronominal head and producing the string (5) which coincides with (1g).

(5)   [[it]   ] is doubted by them [that you will go]
         N NP   S

Thus the first analysis differentiates (1f) from (1g) in terms of the relative ordering of the transformation deleting the pronominal head of the noun phrase complement construction and the passive transformation. The former precedes the latter in the derivation of (1f). The latter precedes the former in the derivation of (1g). Furthermore, this derivation of (1g) presupposes that the extraposition transformation follows the passive transformation in application. If the contrary were true, then we should have no mechanism capable of producing the string (5) after the

passive transformation gives us (4b). The ordering of the passive transformation with respect to extraposition is also a feature of the second
alternative analysis which we now explore.

In the second analysis, the derivations of (1f) and (1g) both depend upon
the application of the passive transformation to the underlying structure
prior to the deletion of the pronominal head of the noun phrase complement sentence. In other words, the string (4b) is an intermediate stage in
the derivation of the two sentences. The subsequent derivation of (1f)
depends upon the deletion of the pronominal head, generating the string
(6).

(6)   [[that you will go]   ] is doubted by them
                          S NP

The derivation of (1g) in this analysis is identical to the derivation proposed in the first analysis, namely, through the application of the extraposition transformation. The differentiation of (1f) and (1g) here has
nothing to do with ordering, as was the case with the first alternative
examined. Rather the differentiation is a result of having applied one of
two transformations, the transformation deleting the pronominal head of
the complement construction, (1f), or the extraposition transformation,
(1g).

Although both formulations seem to be adequate with respect to the data
thus far examined, the consequences of these formulations are not identical with respect to other aspects of the object complement system.
More specifically, consider the following sentences (8) in which the object complement is followed by a prepositional phrase in the underlying
structure (7).

(7)   [NP   AUX   V   [DET   N   S]   [PREP   NP]   ]
                               NP   PP S

(8)   a.   nobody expected it of John that he could be so cruel

      b.   nobody expected of John that he could be so cruel

      c.   *nobody expected that he could be so cruel of John

What these sentences indicate is that the pronominal head of the complement construction cannot in this particular instance be deleted before
the application of the extraposition transformation since such deletion
permits the derivation of (8c). But this fact presents grave difficulties
for the first formulation when considered with regard to the possible
passive versions of the sentences in (8).

(9)   a.   it wasn't expected of John that he could be so cruel

      b.   that he could be so cruel wasn't expected of John

The derivation of sentence (9a) is perfectly straightforward. The passive
transformation, which we already know must precede the extraposition
transformation in order of application, applies to the string (10) to yield

the string (11) upon which the extraposition transformation subsequently applies to produce the string (12).

(10)   nobody expected [it [that he could be so cruel]   ]   [of John]
                                              S NP   PP

(11)   [it [that he could be so cruel]   ] was expected [of John] by nobody
                                S NP   PP

(12)   [it] was expected [of John] by nobody [that he could be so cruel]
        NP   PP   S

The major problem arises in the derivation of (9b). If it is the case that extraposition is obligatory for noun phrase complements in the object position of this construction, and if extraposition is dependent upon the existence of the pronominal head of the complement construction, and if the extraposition transformation follows the passive transformation, it appears that the pronominal head cannot be deleted prior to the application of the passive transformation. For if this deletion were to occur prior to the application of the passive transformation, which we recall is optional, and if the passive was subsequently not applied, the grammar should then have generated the ungrammatical sentence (8c).

What all of this means is that the source of the passive sentence (9b) could not have been simply the phrase "that he could be so cruel." Rather, since the pronominal head cannot be deleted prior to the application of the passive transformation, this passive sentence must have originated from the structure formalized as [it [that John could be so cruel]   ].
        S NP

In other words, the derivation of (9b) must follow the second formulation given earlier in which the first two stages of the derivation are identical to those specified in (10) and (11). But in this case, the extraposition transformation is not applied to the output, thereby yielding (9a); rather, the pronominal head of the complement construction is deleted, correctly giving (9b). What this demonstrates is that the first alternative formulation of the rules for characterizing the derivation of (1f) and (1g) does not generalize to other data that the grammar must cover. The second formulation succeeds where the first fails and, for this reason, is to be preferred. Consequently, we can specify the partial derivation of the sentences (1f) and (1g) as follows:[2]

(13)   Sentence (1f)

First Cycle—no operations

they doubt [[it]   [you will go]   ] [by + P]   BASE
              N   S NP   MAN

Second Cycle

they doubt [[it]   [that you will go]   ] [by + P] T_{CP}
              N   S NP   MAN

[[it]   [that you will go]   ]   be + en doubt [by + them] T_P
 N   S NP   MAN

[[it]   [that you will go]   ]   be doubt + en [by + them] T_{AUX}
 N   S NP   MAN

[[that you will go]   ]   be doubt + en [by + them] T_{PD}
          S NP   MAN

Post Cycle

[[that you will go]   ]   is doubted [by + them]   M
          S NP   MAN

(14)   Sentence (1g)

First Cycle—no operations

they doubt [[it]   [you will go]   ]   [by + P]   BASE
          N   S NP   MAN

Second Cycle

they doubt [[it]   [that you will go]   ]   [by + P] T_{CP}
          N   S NP   MAN

[[it]   [that you will go]   ]   be + en doubt [by + them] T_P
 N   S NP   MAN

[[it]   ] be + en doubt [by + them]   [that you will go] T_E
 N NP   MAN   S

[[it]   ] be doubt + en [by + them]   [that you will go] T_{AUX}
 N NP   MAN   S

Post Cycle

[[it]   ] is doubted [by + them]   [that you will go]   M
 N NP   MAN   S

Directing attention now to the optional deletion of the complementizer "that," we find evidence suggesting that any rule proposed to account for this phenomenon must follow the extraposition transformation. Consider the following data:

(15) a.   1.   it is strange that John isn't here
          2.   it is strange John isn't here

      b.   1.   it happens that John discovered the same thing yesterday
          2.   it happens John discovered the same thing yesterday

On the supposition that a "that" deletion transformation precedes the extraposition transformation, we should have to account for the fact that if this rule does apply, the extraposition transformation is always obligatory if the complement construction is in sentence initial position.

(16) a.   1.   that you will find him is doubted by them
          2.   it is doubted by them that you will find him
          3.   *you will find him is doubted by them

    b.   1.   that you were broke was known by everybody
           2.   it was known by everybody that you were broke
           3.   *you were broke was known by everybody

To explain the nonoccurrence of sentences (16a. 3, 16b. 3) requires, first of all, that the extraposition transformation be divided into an optional case and an obligatory case and, second, that the obligatory version be sensitive to more structure than simply the contiguity of the pronominal head of the complement construction with the complement sentence itself. In particular, this statement must list information about the constituency of the complement sentence, namely, that the complementizer "that" is no longer in the structure. There are many difficulties connected with this proposal which require no elaboration here since the greatly increased cost of this formulation over the one in which a "that" deletion transformation follows the extraposition transformation is sufficient to exclude this proposal from further consideration.

Although the ordering of the "that" deletion transformation (henceforth case "b" of the optional complementizer deletion transformation, T_{OCD}) following the extraposition transformation is necessary to explain the nonoccurrence of the ungrammatical sentences in (16), the precise formulation of this transformation presents certain difficulties. Consider these sentences:

(17)   a.   1.   I doubt that John came yesterday quite seriously
              2.   I doubt John came yesterday quite seriously
              3.   I doubt quite seriously that John came yesterday
              4.   *I doubt quite seriously John came yesterday

        b.   1.   nobody expected (it) of John that he could be so cruel
              2.   *nobody expected (it) of John he could be so cruel

        c.   1.   it is important to John that you are here on time
              2.   *it is important to John you are here on time

        d.   1.   I convinced Bill that John was not so bad
              2.   I convinced Bill John was not so bad

These data suggest that the deletion of the complementizer "that" may be restricted to only those instances where this complementizer immediately follows either the verb with an NP intervening optionally or the predicate adjective in the main sentence.[3] According to this restriction, the grammar would correctly predict the deletion of the "that" in the following instances:

(18)   a.   1.   I think that John is coming
              2.   I think John is coming

        b.   1.   it is strange that John came late
              2.   it is strange John came late

Certain dialectal phenomena suggest that the transformation deleting indefinite pronouns, which has been discussed in the literature[4] but not listed in Chapter 1, must follow the extraposition transformation but must precede case "b" of T_{OCD}. In these dialects, the following deletions of the complementizer "that" are encountered:

(19) a. 1. it was thought by someone that you would come
          2. *it was thought by someone you would come
          3. it was thought that you would come
          4. it was thought you would come

      b. 1. it is important to someone that you do it
          2. *it is important to someone you do it
          3. it is important that you do it
          4. it is important you do it

The sentences (19a. 2, b. 2) are ungrammatical and are prevented by the fact that case "b" of T_{OCD} is not defined on these strings. Since the appropriate environment is not met in these sentences, the deletion of the complementizer "that" is impossible. However, if the transformation deleting the indefinite "someone" in (19) is ordered to apply prior to the application of case "b" of T_{OCD}, then the "that" complementizer, now contiguous with the verb or predicate adjective, can be deleted optionally.

In the past few pages, we have been exploring the form and order of application of the transformational rules required to generate the sentences in paradigm (1). Specifically, we have seen that, aside from the complementizer placement transformation, T_{CP}, five transformations are necessary. These are the passive transformation, the extraposition transformation, the pronoun deletion transformation, case "b" of the optional complementizer deletion transformation, and the indefinite pronoun deletion transformation. It has been proposed, furthermore, that four of these rules are critically ordered as follows:

1.   Passive Transformation—T_P

2.   Extraposition Transformation—T_E

3.   Indefinite Pronoun Deletion Transformation—unlisted

4.   Optional Complementizer Deletion Transformation—
     T_{OCD} (case "b")

The last issue to be discussed before the derivation of the sentences in the paradigm (1) can be fully specified concerns the ordering of the transformation deleting the pronominal head (henceforth to be identified as the pronoun deletion transformation as defined in Chapter 1). The central question has to do with whether the pronoun deletion transformation precedes or follows the extraposition transformation. Two options present themselves: First, pronoun deletion is optional and precedes extraposition which is obligatory. Second, pronoun deletion is obligatory and follows extraposition which is optional. There is evidence suggesting that the second alternative is preferable to the first, but let us consider both alternatives in slightly greater detail.

The first alternative can be illuminated in terms of the following data:

(20) a. 1. that you could do such a thing bothers me
          2. it bothers me that you could do such a thing

      b. 1. I didn't suspect that you would fail for a moment
          2. I didn't suspect for a moment that you would fail

In the first analysis, the nonapplication of the optional pronoun deletion transformation produces the sentences (20a. 2, b. 2), since the extraposition transformation is obligatory. If the former rule does apply, then the sentences (20a. 1, b. 1) will be generated since the necessary environment for the application of the extraposition transformation is not satisfied. The central difficulty with this analysis stems from the fact that the extraposition transformation may apply vacuously, as in a base string like (21).

(21) I think [[it]   [that John is leaving]   ]
              N   S NP

Since the variable Y in the extraposition transformation as stated in Chapter 1 may be null, it follows that the extraposition transformation, which we recall is obligatory in this analysis, will apply with a resulting alteration of the constituent structure. In particular, the vacuous application of the extraposition transformation will take the complement sentence from under the domination of the NP and attach it to some higher constituent, perhaps S. We observe, however, that the application of the extraposition transformation has no effect on the linear sequence of the constituents in the structural description if the variable Y is null. Since it still remains necessary, therefore, to delete the pronominal head, the first analysis must include an additional pronominal deletion rule just to cover the cases in which the extraposition transformation applies vacuously.

It is not necessary to posit two pronominal deletion transformations for exactly the same purpose in the second formulation for here an optional extraposition transformation precedes an obligatory pronoun deletion transformation. In this analysis, the nonapplication of the extraposition transformation necessitates the application of the pronoun deletion transformation, thus generating the sentences (20a. 1, b. 1). If the extraposition transformation does apply, then the sentences (20a. 2, b. 2) are correctly generated. Finally, in the event that the extraposition transformation applies vacuously, as in (21), the pronoun deletion transformation applies obligatorily to yield (22).

(22) I think that John is leaving

We thus conclude that the pronoun deletion transformation is obligatory and follows the extraposition transformation which is optional.

There is a special case of pronoun deletion which is optional in many instances. Consider, for example, the following sentences:

(23)   a.   1.   I dislike it very much that he is always late
            2.   I dislike very much that he is always late

       b.   1.   I didn't suspect it for a moment that you would fail
            2.   I didn't suspect for a moment that you would fail

       c.   1.   I believe it to be true that oculists are eye doctors
            2.   *I believe to be true that oculists are eye doctors

Although there are many unanswered questions about the restrictions on
pronominal deletions of the sort exemplified by the sentences in (23), it
appears that it is necessary to postulate a variation of the pronoun deletion transformation that is occasionally optional and allows for the deletion of the pronominal head just in case an adverbial intercedes between
the pronoun and the complement sentence. This is case "b" of T_{PD} as
defined in Chapter 1.

There is little evidence allowing us to decide whether the pronoun deletion transformation, which follows the extraposition transformation, must
precede or follow case "b" of T_{OCD}. There seems to be no particular
problem with postulating that the deletion of the complementizer "that"
precedes the pronoun deletion transformation. In such a formulation, we
observe that the deletion of "that" depends upon the vacuous application
of the extraposition transformation. We observe that case "b" of T_{OCD}
is not defined upon strings like (24).

(24)   a.   I think [[it]   [that John is coming]   ]
                   N   S NP

       b.   I imagined [[it]   [that my boat sank in the hurricane]   ]
                        N   S NP

This follows from the fact that the pronominal head is not an NP, but an N.
The application of the extraposition transformation to these strings results, however, in an environment upon which case "b" of T_{OCD} is
defined.

(25)   a.   I think [[it]   ]   [that John is coming]
                   N NP   S

       b.   I imagined [[it]   ]   [that my boat sank in the hurricane]
                        N NP   S

The basic virtue of this analysis is that, as we shall see in the following
discussion, it becomes possible to collapse, albeit only partially, the
"that" deletion rule with the rules that optionally delete "for" and
"POSS." But this is anything but conclusive justification for the analysis.

The order required for the application of the transformations discussed
thus far is as follows:

1.   Passive Transformation—T_P

2.   Extraposition Transformation—T_E

3.   Indefinite Pronoun Deletion Transformation—unlisted

4.   Optional Complementizer Deletion Transformation—T_{OCDb}

5.   Pronoun Deletion Transformation—T_{PD}

On the basis of these transformations, plus the auxiliary transformation, the derivation of the sentences (1a)-(1e) in the paradigm may be specified in the following manner:

(26)   Sentence (1a)

First Cycle—no operations

they doubt [[it]   [you will go]   ]   BASE
        N   S NP

Second Cycle

they doubt [[it]   [that you will go]   ] T_{CP}
        N   S NP

(27)   Sentence (1b)

First Cycle—no operations

they doubt [[it]   [you will go]   ]   BASE
        N   S NP

Second Cycle

they doubt [[it]   [that you will go]   ] T_{CP}
        N   S NP

they doubt [[that you will go]   ] T_{PD}
                        S NP

(28)   Sentence (1c)

First Cycle—no operations

they doubt [[it]   [you will go]   ]   BASE
        N   S NP

Second Cycle

they doubt [[it]   [that you will go]   ] T_{CP}
        N   S NP

they doubt [[it]   ]   [that you will go] T_E
        N NP   S

they doubt [[it]   ]   [you will go] T_{OCDb}
        N NP   S

they doubt [you will go] T_{PD}
                S

(29)   Sentence (1d)

First Cycle—no operations

they doubt [[it]   [you will go]   ]   [very much]   BASE
        N   S NP   ADV

Second Cycle

they doubt [[it]   [that you will go]   ]   [very much] T_{CP}
        N   S NP   ADV

they doubt [[it]   ]   [very much]   [that you will go] T_E
        N NP   ADV   S

The derivation of sentence (1e) requires the application of case "b" of T_{PD} to generate the following string:

they doubt [very much]   [that you will go] T_{PDb}
            ADV   S

4. 1. 2.   The "POSS-ing" complementizer

Object complement constructions containing the "POSS-ing" complementizer are similar in certain respects to those constructions containing the "that" complementizer but are sufficiently different nonetheless to warrant consideration. Compared with paradigm (1), the paradigm for the "POSS-ing" object complement constructions is quite impoverished.

(30)   a.   *everybody prefers it your driving slowly

       b.   everybody prefers your driving slowly

       c.   everybody prefers you driving slowly

       d.   *everybody prefers it very much your driving slowly

       e.   *everybody prefers very much your driving slowly

       f.   your driving slowly is preferred by everybody

       g.   *it is preferred by everybody your driving slowly

One of the more striking aspects of the restrictions on the sentences in this paradigm is the fact that the pronominal head of the object complement cannot occur. This should not be taken as evidence that these sentences are not instances of noun phrase complementation. We are advised of the spuriousness of this conclusion by the existence of the pseudocleft sentences in (31).

(31)   a.   what everybody prefers is your driving slowly

       b.   what is preferred by everybody is your driving slowly

It would seem more correct to say that the pronominal head of the complement construction is obligatorily deleted just in case the complementizer in the complement sentences happens to be "POSS-ing."

In addition to the fact that the deletion of the pronominal head is obligatory in such constructions, it is also observed that extraposition is, in
general, impossible—a fact exemplified by (30d, e, g). This suggests that
if the extraposition transformation is so restricted that it cannot apply
in the event that the complementizer of the complement sentence following the pronominal head is "POSS-ing," then the obligatory deletion of
the pronominal head becomes an automatic consequence of the pronoun
deletion transformation. In other words, by preventing the application of
the extraposition transformation, we bring about the obligatory deletion
of the pronoun. Thus, the string (30a) must become the string (30b).

In addition to the nonextraposition and obligatory pronoun deletion which
we observe in (29), we notice that the "POSS" segment of the "POSS-ing"
complementizer can be optionally deleted, as in (29c). Superficially, this
deletion would appear describable as a special instance of case "b" of
the optional complementizer deletion transformation, T_{OCD}, which
asserts that the "that" complementizer can be optionally deleted when it
follows the verb or predicate adjective immediately. Certain other considerations suggest that this simplification is specious. Consider what
the following examples demonstrate:

(32) a. 1. I convinced Mary that he was honest
          2. I convinced Mary he was honest

      b. 1. I convinced Mary of his being honest
          2. *I convinced Mary of him being honest

We recall that case "b" of T_{OCD} is defined over a verb or adjective followed by an optional noun phrase followed by "that." If the data in (32) is
representative, it is observed that the deletion of the complementizer
"POSS" is impossible in the event that an NP intervenes between the complementizer and the verb. This suggests the necessity of establishing a
second case of the optional complementizer deletion transformation in
order to handle the "POSS" complementizer. In other words, we should
establish a two-case transformation like the following:

$$(33) \quad X \quad \begin{Bmatrix} V \\ ADJ \end{Bmatrix} \quad \begin{Bmatrix} a. & \emptyset \\ b. & (NP) \end{Bmatrix} \quad \begin{Bmatrix} a. & \begin{bmatrix} +C \\ +D \\ +E \end{bmatrix} \\ b. & \begin{bmatrix} +C \\ -D \end{bmatrix} \end{Bmatrix} \quad Y$$

$$1 \qquad 2 \qquad\qquad 3 \qquad\qquad 4 \qquad\qquad 5 \Longrightarrow 1, 2, 3, \emptyset, 5$$

Looking ahead to the "for-to" object complement constructions, we discover that case "a" in (32) can be significantly simplified. Consider the
following sentences:

(34) a. 1. I would hate for John to lose it
          2. I would hate John to lose it

      b. 1. I would hate very much for John to lose it
          2. *I would hate very much John to lose it

    c. 1. for you to stay here would be impossible
        2. *you to stay here would be impossible

    d. 1. it was important for you to do that
        2. *it was important you to do that

    e. 1. I was embarrassed for you to see the mess
        2. *I was embarrassed you to see the mess

    f. 1. preferring for John to leave is not nice
        2. preferring John to leave is not nice

The simplest description of the restrictions on the optional deletion of
the complementizer "for" seems to be the following: The complementizer "for" may be optionally deleted just in case this complementizer
follows the pronominal head of the complement construction, which itself
follows the verb in the main sentence. In other words, we propose a
transformation somewhat like the following:

$$
(35) \quad X \quad \left\{ \begin{matrix} V \\ ADJ \end{matrix} \right\} \quad \begin{matrix} N \\ [+PRO] \end{matrix} \quad \left[\begin{matrix} +C \\ +D \\ -E \end{matrix} \right] \quad Y
$$

$$
\quad\quad 1 \quad\quad\quad 2 \quad\quad\quad\quad 3 \quad\quad\quad\quad 4 \quad\quad\quad\quad\quad 5 \Longrightarrow 1, 2, 3, \emptyset, 5
$$

The essential difference between case "a" in (33) and (35) is that (33a)
does not require an intervening pronoun between the complementizer and
the verb or adjective.[5] Since there are no unfortunate consequences from
allowing a pronoun to intervene in case "b" of (33), it becomes possible
to generalize the special cases of the optional complementizer deletion
rule which handle "POSS" deletion and "for" deletion in terms of a single
rule, namely, case "a" of the optional complementizer deletion rule as
defined in Chapter 1. Since only two complementizing features, [+C][+D],
are sufficient to characterize both the "for-to" complementizer and the
"POSS-ing" complementizer, the generalization of the rules that delete
these items represents a significant improvement on any formulation of
these rules in which three distinct cases are postulated.[6]

This brings us to the last transformation required to derive the sentences in the paradigm (30), the auxiliary transformation which inverts the
"POSS" complementizer with the initial NP of the complement sentence
and the "ing" complementizer with V, have, or be. The ordering of the
auxiliary transformation is crucial. If we claim that the auxiliary transformation precedes the optional complementizer deletion transformation
in order of application, it then becomes necessary to postulate a much
more complex optional complementizer deletion rule. The reason for
this is that if the auxiliary transformation applies, then the environments
of the "POSS" and "for" are no longer the same. More specifically, the
"for" still precedes the subject noun phrase of the complement sentence,
but the "POSS" complementizer now follows the subject noun phrase as
a consequence of the application of the auxiliary transformation. Thus

we should have to propose a transformation of roughly the following form:[7]

$$(36) \quad X \quad V \quad \begin{array}{c} N \\ [+PRO] \end{array} \left(\begin{bmatrix} +C \\ +D \\ -E \end{bmatrix}\right) \quad NP \quad \left(\begin{bmatrix} +C \\ +D \\ +E \end{bmatrix}\right) \quad Y$$

$$1 \quad 2 \quad 3 \quad 4 \quad 5 \quad 6 \quad 7 \Longrightarrow 1, 2, 3, \emptyset, 5, \emptyset$$

Since the optional complementizer deletion transformation, T_{OCD}, is considerably less complex if the auxiliary transformation follows it in order of application (since both complementizers are in the same environment before the application of the auxiliary transformation), this ordering is to be preferred.

A brief summary will, perhaps, be helpful at this point. We have established the necessity of the following ordered set of transformations:

1.   Passive Transformation—T_P

2.   Extraposition Transformation—T_E

3.   Indefinite Pronoun Deletion Transformation—unlisted

4.   Optional Complementizer Deletion Transformation—T_{OCD}

5.   Auxiliary Transformation—T_{AUX}

6.   Pronoun Deletion Transformation—T_{PD}

On the basis of the foregoing discussion, the derivations of the sentences in the paradigm (30) may be specified in the following fashion:

(37)   Sentence (30b)

First Cycle—no operations

everybody prefers [[it] [[you] [drive slowly]]]   BASE
               N   NP   VP S NP

Second Cycle

everybody prefers [[it] [POSS[you] [ing drive slowly]]] T_{CP}
               N   NP   VP S NP

everybody prefers [[it] [[you + POSS] [drive + ing slowly]]] T_{AUX}
               N   NP   VP S NP

everybody prefers [[[you + POSS] [drive + ing slowly]]] T_{PDa}
                    NP   VP S NP

Post Cycle

everybody prefers [[[your] [driving slowly]]]   M
                 NP   VP S NP

(38)   Sentence (30c)

First Cycle—no operations

everybody prefers [[it]   [[you]   [drive slowly]   ]   ]   BASE
            N   NP   VP S NP

Second Cycle

everybody prefers [[it]   [POSS [you]   [ing drive slowly]   ]   ] T_{CP}
            N   NP   VP S NP

everybody prefers [[it]   [[you]   [ing drive slowly]   ]   ] T_{OCD}
            N   NP   VP S NP

everybody prefers [[it]   [[you]   [drive + ing slowly]   ]   ] T_{AUX}
            N   NP   VP S NP

everybody prefers [[[you]   [drive + ing slowly]   ]   ] T_{PDa}
               NP   VP S NP

Post Cycle

everybody prefers [[[you]   [driving slowly]   ]   ]   M
               NP   VP S NP

(39)   Sentence (30)

First Cycle—no operations

everybody prefers [[it]   [[you]   [drive slowly]   ]   ]   BASE
            N   NP   VP S NP

Second Cycle

everybody prefers [[it]   [POSS [you]   [ing drive slowly]   ]   ]
            N   NP   VP S NP

[by + P] T_{CP}
 MAN

[[it]   [POSS [you]   [ing drive slowly]   ]   ] be + en prefer
 N   NP   VP S NP

[by + everybody] T_P
       MAN

[[it]   [[you + POSS]   [drive + ing slowly]   ]   ] be prefer + en
 N   NP   VP S NP

[by + everybody] T_{AUX}
       MAN

[[[you + POSS]   [drive + ing slowly]   ]   ] be prefer + en
     NP   VP S NP

[by + everybody] T_{PD}
       MAN

Post Cycle

[[[your]   [driving slowly]   ]   ] is preferred [by + everybody]   M
   NP   VP S NP   MAN

Let us now consider the sentences in paradigm (40), where the identity erasure transformation has applied to delete the subject noun phrase of the complement sentence.

(40) a. everybody prefers driving slowly

     b. driving slowly is preferred by everybody

Certain considerations strongly suggest that the identity erasure transformation must precede the passive transformation in order of application. As evidence supporting this contention, consider the following sentences:

(41) a. Bill reminded them to greet me

     b. they were reminded by Bill to greet me

As we shall see later, these sentences are instances of noun phrase complementation having the underlying structure given in (42).

(42)

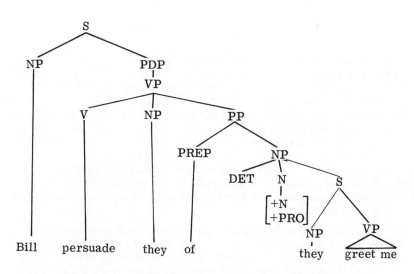

It is observed that if the identity erasure transformation applies prior to the application of the passive transformation, that is, directly to the structure given in (42), then the noun phrase "they" in the complement sentence is correctly erased by the object noun phrase "they" in the main sentence. Let us suppose, however, that the identity erasure transformation does not apply until after the passive transformation, that is, on a derived structure which has roughly the form shown in diagram (43).

(43)

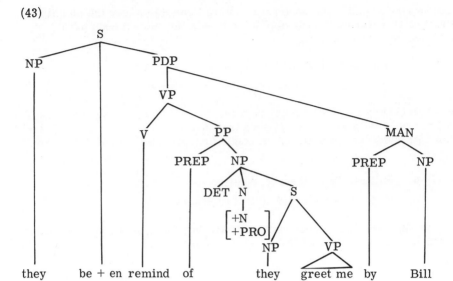

We observe that the erasure principle operates incorrectly with respect
to the derived structure (43). In particular, the initial NP in the complement sentence, "they," is closer to the NP in the agentive phrase "by +
Bill" than it is to the subject of the derived main sentence, "they." It thus
becomes extremely difficult to explain the identity of the deleted NP in
the complement sentence with the derived subject of the main sentence.
At best, it would become necessary to propose considerable modification
of the erasure principle. At worst, the conditions governing deletion
could not be stated at all. This difficulty is completely resolved by requiring the identity erasure transformation to apply before the passive
transformation since, as we see in (42), erasure is correctly defined at
this stage of a derivation.

Finally, we consider the ordering of the complementizer placement
transformation with respect to the identity erasure transformation. Although the evidence is not overwhelming, there is some reason to suppose
that the complementizer placement transformation precedes the identity
erasure transformation. We recall that identity erasure is possible just
in case the complementizer is either "for-to" or "POSS-ing." If the complementizer is "that," then identity erasure does not apply. If we assume
that the identity erasure transformation applies before the complementizer placement transformation, it then becomes necessary to insure that
the former will not apply in the event that the complementizer introduced subsequently by the complementizer placement transformation is
"that." This can be accomplished, perhaps, by specifying that the variable X which intervenes between the NP to the left of the complement
sentence in the structural description does not include any segment

which is marked $[-D]$. In other words, we might revise the formulation of the identity erasure transformation as follows:

(44)   U   (NP)   X   [NP Y] W (NP) Z
$$\qquad\qquad\qquad\qquad\text{not}\,[\alpha,[-D],\beta]\qquad\quad \text{S}$$

     1   2   3   4 5 6   7   8$\Longrightarrow$

    (i)   2 is erased by 4

    (ii) 7 is erased by 4

This formulation is probably adequate for all instances where the complementizer allowed by the verb or adjective in the main sentence is exclusively "that." But this formulation will not work where all three complementizer options are possible, as in (45).

(45)   a.   I dislike it that he is so cruel

       b.   I dislike it for him to be so cruel

       c.   I dislike his being so cruel

In cases like (45), the pronominal head will be marked simply $[+C]$ since all complementizer options are possible. Thus the restriction imposed on the variable X in (44) will not be sufficient to block the application of the identity erasure transformation in (45), and an ungrammatical sentence will result. There well may be some way in which the identity erasure transformation can be formulated to prevent the erasure of an NP in the complement sentence when the complementizer placement transformation follows the identity erasure transformation. For present purposes, it seems a good deal simpler to propose that the complementizer placement transformation precedes the identity erasure transformation. Since the former marks complement sentences, it becomes possible to define identity erasure in terms of the complementizer structure assigned by the complementizer placement transformation. In other words, for the application of the identity erasure transformation it is sufficient to know only that the introduced complementizer is either "for" or "POSS," $[+C][+D]$. In this formulation it is clearly unnecessary to impose any restrictions on the variable X in the structural description for the identity erasure transformation.

The following ordered set of transformations is thus proposed:

1.   Complementizer Placement Transformation—T_{CP}

2.   Identity Erasure Transformation—T_{IE}

3.   Passive Transformation—T_P

4.   Extraposition Transformation—T_E

5.   Indefinite Pronoun Deletion Transformation—unlisted

6.   Optional Complementizer Deletion Transformation—T_{OCD}

7.   Auxiliary Transformation—T_{AUX}

8.   Pronoun Deletion Transformation—T_{PD}

On the basis of this set of transformational rules plus the obligatory complementizer deletion transformation, the motivation and ordering of which will be discussed shortly, we can specify the derivation of the sentences in (39) in the following fashion.

(46)   Sentence (40)

First Cycle—no operations

everybody prefers [[it] [[everybody] [drive slowly]]]   BASE
              N   NP   VP S NP

Second Cycle

everybody prefers [[it] [POSS [everybody] [ing drive slowly]]] T_{CP}
            NP   NP   VP S NP

everybody prefers [[it] [POSS [ing drive slowly]]] T_{IE}
              N   VP S NP

everybody prefers [[it] [POSS [drive + ing slowly]]] T_{AUX}
              N   VP S NP

everybody prefers [[POSS [drive + ing slowly]]] T_{PD}
                             VP S NP

everybody prefers [[[drive + ing slowly]]] T_{CD}
                        VP S NP

Post Cycle

everybody prefers [[[driving slowly]]]   M
                      VP S NP

(47)   Sentence (40b)

First Cycle—no operations

everybody prefers [[it] [[everybody] [drive slowly]]] [by + P] BASE
              N   NP   VP S NP   MAN

Second Cycle

everybody prefers [[it] [POSS [everybody] [ing drive slowly]]]
              N   NP   VP S NP
[by + P] T_{CP}
  MAN

everybody prefers [[it] [POSS [ing drive slowly]]] [by + P] T_{IE}
              N   VP S NP   MAN

[[it] [POSS [ing drive slowly]]] be + en prefer [by + everybody] T_P
  N   VP S NP   MAN

[[it] [POSS [drive + ing slowly]]] be prefer + en
  N   VP S NP
[by + everybody] T_{AUX}
       MAN

[[POSS [drive + ing slowly]]] be prefer + en [by + everybody]   T$_{PD}$
        VP S NP   MAN

[[[drive + ing slowly]]] be prefer + en [by + everybody]   T$_{CD}$
        VP S NP   MAN

Post Cycle

[[[driving slowly]]] is preferred [by + everybody]   M
      VP S NP   MAN

4.1.3. The "for-to" complementizer

The paradigms listing the basic object complement constructions with "for-to" are far more complete than the paradigms for the "POSS-ing" complementizer because the extraposition transformation is not restricted with respect to the "for-to" complementizer. This difference notwithstanding, the set of transformations just summarized for similar constructions with the "POSS-ing" and the "that" complementizers is fully capable of handling the derivations of all sentences in the "for-to" paradigm.[8]

(48) a. everyone would prefer it for you to come early

    b. everyone would prefer for you to come early

    c. everyone would prefer you to come early

    d. everyone would prefer it very much for you to come early

    e. everyone would prefer very much for you to come early

    f. it would be preferred by everyone for you to come early

    g. for you to come early would be preferred by everyone

(49) a. everyone would prefer it to come early

    b. everyone would prefer to come early

    c. everyone would prefer very much to come early

    d. to come early would be preferred by everyone

    e. it would be preferred by everyone to come early

In terms of the set of transformations proposed earlier, the derivations of the sentences in the paradigms may be specified in the following manner:

(50) Sentence (48a)

First Cycle—no operations

everyone would prefer [[it] [[you] [come early]]]   BASE
                 N   NP   VP S NP

Second Cycle

everyone would prefer [[it] [for [you] [to come early]]]   T$_{CP}$
                 N   NP   VP S NP

(51) Sentence (48b)

First Cycle—no operations

everyone would prefer [[it] [[you] [come early]]]   BASE
                 N   NP   VP S NP

Second Cycle

everyone would prefer [[it] [for [you] [to + come early]]] T$_{CP}$
                 N   NP   VP S NP

everyone would prefer [[for [you] [to come early]]]   T$_{PD}$
                      NP   VP S NP

(52) Sentence (48c)

First Cycle—no operations

everyone would prefer [[it] [[you] [come early]]]   BASE
                 N   NP   VP S NP

Second Cycle

everyone would prefer [[it] [for [you] [to come early]]]   T$_{CP}$
                 N   NP   VP S NP

everyone would prefer [[it] [[you] [to come early]]]   T$_{OCD}$
                 N   NP   VP S NP

everyone would prefer [[[you] [to come early]]]   T$_{PD}$
                   NP   VP S NP

(53) Sentence (48d)

First Cycle—no operations

everyone would prefer [[it] [[you] [come early]]] very much] BASE
                 N   NP   VP S NP   ADV

Second Cycle

everyone would prefer [[it] [for [you] [to come early]]]
                 N   NP   VP S NP
[very much]   T$_{CP}$
  ADV

everyone would prefer [[it]] [very much] [for [you]
                 N NP   ADV   NP
[to come early]]   T$_E$
  VP S

In the derivation of (48e), case "b" of T$_{PD}$ applies to the string just above.

everyone would prefer [very much] [for [you] [to come early]] T$_{PDb}$
                         ADV   NP   VP S

(54) Sentence (48f)

First Cycle—no operations

everyone would prefer [[it] [[you] [come early]]] [by + P]   BASE
              N   NP   VP   S   NP   MAN

Second Cycle

everyone would prefer [[it] [for [you] [to come early]]]
              N   NP   VP   S   NP
[by + P] T_{CP}
    MAN

[[it] [for [you] [to come early]]] would be + en prefer
  N   NP   VP   S   NP
[by + everybody] T_P
       MAN

[[it]] would be + en prefer [by + everybody] [for [you]
  N   NP   MAN   NP
[to come early]] T_E
     VP   S

[[it]] would be prefer + en [by + everybody] [for [you]
  N   NP   MAN   NP
[to come early]] T_{AUX}
     VP   S

Post Cycle

[[it]] would be preferred [by + everybody] [for [you]
  N   NP   MAN   NP
[to come early]]   M
     VP   S

(55) Sentence (48g)

First Cycle—no operations

everyone would prefer [[it] [[you] [come early]]] [by + P]   BASE
              N   NP   VP   S   NP   MAN

Second Cycle

everyone would prefer [it] [for [you] [to come early]]]
             N   NP   VP   S   NP
[by + P] T_{CP}
    MAN

[[it] [for [you] [to come early]]] would be + en prefer
  N   NP   VP   S   NP
[by + everybody] T_P
       MAN

[[it] [for [you] [to come early]]] would be prefer + en
  N   NP   VP   S   NP
[by + everybody] T_{AUX}
       MAN

```
[[for [you]  [to come early]  ]  ] would be prefer + en
      NP           VP S NP
[by + everybody]                                              T_PDa
        MAN
```

Post Cycle

```
[[for [you]  [to come early]  ]  ] would be preferred
      NP           VP S NP
[by + everybody]                                              M
        MAN
```

(56)   Sentence (49a)

First Cycle—no operations

```
everyone would prefer [[it]  [[everyone]  [come early]  ]  ]      BASE
                        N        NP          VP S NP
```

Second Cycle

```
everyone would prefer [[it]  [for [everyone]  [to come early]  ]  ]  T_CP
                        N          NP            VP S NP
```

```
everyone would prefer [[it]  [for [to come early]  ]  ]           T_IE
                        N           VP S NP
```

```
everyone would prefer [[it]  [[to come early]  ]  ]              T_CD
                        N        VP S NP
```

If T_{PD} had applied in the derivation just above, the grammar would have generated sentence (49b).

```
everyone would prefer [[[to come early]  ]  ]                   T_PD
                          VP S NP
```

(57)   Sentence (49c)

First Cycle—no operations

```
everyone would prefer [[it]  [[everyone]  [come early]  ]  ]
                        N        NP          VP S NP
[very much]                                                   BASE
   ADV
```

Second Cycle

```
everyone would prefer [[it]  [for [everyone]  [to come early]  ]  ]
                        N          NP            VP S NP
[very much]                                                   T_CP
   ADV
```

```
everyone would prefer [[it]  [for [to come early]  ]  ] [very much]  T_IE
                        N           VP S NP                 ADV
```

```
everyone would prefer [[it]  ] [very much] [for [to come early]  ]  T_E
                        N NP      ADV            VP S
```

everyone would prefer [[it]   ] [very much] [[to come early]   ] T_{CD}
             N NP   ADV   VP S

In the derivation of (49d), case "b" of T_{PD} applies to the string just above.

everyone would prefer [very much] [[to come early]   ] T_{PDb}
                 ADV   VP S

(58) Sentence (49e)

First Cycle—no operations

everyone would prefer [[it] [[everyone] [come early]]]
             N   NP   VP S NP

[by + P]   BASE
  MAN

Second Cycle

everyone would prefer [[it] [for [everyone] [to come early]]]
             N   NP   VP S NP

[by + P] T_{CP}
  MAN

everyone would prefer [[it] [for [to come early]]] [by + P] T_{IE}
             N   VP S NP   MAN

[[it] [for [to come early]]] would be + en prefer [by + everybody] T_P
 N   VP S NP   MAN

[[it]   ] would be + en prefer [by + everybody] [for [to come early]] T_E
 N NP   MAN   VP S

[[it]   ] would be prefer + en [by + everybody] [for [to come early]]
 N NP   MAN   VP S
                                              T_{AUX}

[[it]   ] would be prefer + en [by + everybody] [[to come early]] T_{CD}
 N NP   MAN   VP S

Post Cycle

[[it]   ] would be preferred [by + everybody] [[to come early]]   M
 N NP   MAN   VP S

(59) Sentence (49f)

First Cycle—no operations

everyone would prefer [[it] [[everyone] [some early]]]
             N   NP   VP S NP

[by + P]   BASE
  MAN

Second Cycle

everyone would prefer [[it] [for [everyone] [to come early]   ]   ]
                     N   NP   VP S NP

[by + P] T_{CP}
 MAN

everyone would prefer [[it] [for [to come early]   ]   ] [by + P] T_{IE}
                     N   VP S NP   MAN

[[it] [for [to come early]   ]   ] would be + en prefer
 N   VP S NP

[by + everybody] T_P
     MAN

[[it] [for [to come early]   ]   ] would be prefer + en
 N   VP S NP

[by + everyone] T_{AUX}
   MAN

[[for [to come early]   ]   ] would be prefer + en [by + everyone] T_{PD}
             VP S NP   MAN

[[[to come early]   ]   ] would be prefer + en [by + everyone] T_{CD}
          VP S NP   MAN

Post Cycle

[[[to come early]   ]   ] would be preferred [by + everyone]   M
          VP S NP   MAN

4.1.4.   General discussion

It will be useful at this point to turn to the analysis of a different paradigm, one involving an instance of object complementation, which raises several important questions.

The paradigm illustrates a class of verbs, including "believe," "suspect," "think," and a great many others, which participates in complement constructions of apparently considerable diversity. We observe, first, that a noun phrase complement analysis must be allowed for the verbs in this class. Consider this paradigm:

(60) a.   I believe that John has convinced Bill

      b.   I believe it with no difficulty that John has convinced Bill

      c.   what I believe is that John has convinced Bill

      d.   that John has convinced Bill is believed by me

      e.   it is believed by me that John has convinced Bill

      f.   what is believed by me is that John has convinced Bill

If we assume that the phrase "that John has convinced Bill" is an instance of noun phrase complementation, then the derivation of the sentences in the paradigm follows as an automatic consequence of the application of the transformational rules discussed earlier. The reader will readily convince himself on this point.

Paradigm (60) does not, however, exhaust the number of constructions in which verbs of the "believe" class may appear. Consider, for example, the following sentences which do not at all appear to be instances of noun phrase complementation.

(61) a. I believe John to have convinced Bill

b. John is believed by me to have convinced Bill

There would appear to be some virtue in the conclusion that the sentences in (61) do not represent cases of noun phrase complementation. In the first place, we observe that a pseudocleft sentence version of (61) is completely ungrammatical.

(62) *what I believe is for John to have convinced Bill

Second, the identity erasure rule does not apply whereas the reflexive rule does.

(63) a. *I believe to have convinced Bill

b. I believe myself to have convinced Bill

These data suggest that the sentences in (61) are not instances of noun phrase complementation, but rather verb phrase complementation, and that it is necessary to posit two distinct underlying structures for all verbs in the class under discussion. But the verb phrase complement analysis for the verb class under discussion is not without serious difficulties also, difficulties that become apparent upon careful consideration of other verb phrase complement constructions. As a paradigm case of transitive verb phrase complementation, consider sentence (64).

(64) I compelled the doctor to examine John

Predictably, if (64) is an instance of verb phrase complementation, the pseudocleft sentence (65) is ungrammatical.

(65) *what I compelled was for the doctor to examine John

As an instance of verb phrase complementation, sentence (64) has roughly the underlying form shown in diagram (66).

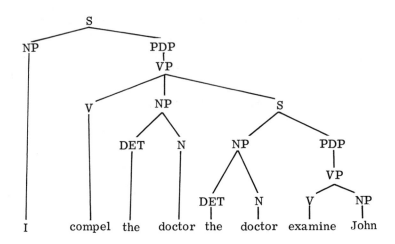

Let us suppose now that the grammar had generated "John" rather than "the doctor" in the object position of the main sentence. If the passive transformation is subsequently applied on the first cycle to the complement sentence in (66), this allows for the derivation of the sentence (67).[9]

(67)   I compelled John to be examined by the doctor

We notice immediately that sentences (64) and (67) have entirely different meanings. I can compel a doctor to examine John without compelling John to be examined by a doctor. The difference in meaning is explained by the grammar by the fact that the two sentences have different underlying structures. In (64), the noun phrase "the doctor" is interpreted as the object of the verb in the underlying structure of the main sentence. In (67), on the other hand, the noun phrase "John" is the object of the verb in the underlying structure. It follows from this discussion that a sentence S_1, with the complement an active sentence derived from a structure like (66), will be synonymous with a sentence S_2, with the complement a passive sentence providing that, all other constituents being identical, the object of the verb in the main sentence of the underlying structure is identical to both the subject and object of the complement sentence in the same underlying structure.

Thus, if the sentences in (68) are instances of verb phrase complementation, it should be the case that passive application to the complement sentence implies a derivation different in meaning from the derivation in which the passive has not applied to the complement sentence. But our prediction is not correct. We observe that the application of the passive transformation does not in the least affect the truth value synonymy of the two sentences.

(68) a. I believe John to have convinced Bill

      b. I believe Bill to have been convinced by John

According to the verb phrase complement analysis, the underlying structures in (68) differ in that the underlying object of "believe" in (68a) is "John" while the underlying object in (68b) is "Bill." The sentences should, therefore, be different in meaning, but they are not. This fact may be taken to mean either that our formulation of transitive verb phrase complementation is incorrect, an event made a priori quite improbable by the precision with which this formulation holds in such a wide range of cases, or that the sentences in (68) are simply not instances of verb phrase complementation.

We are thus led full circle back to the consideration of the sentences in (68) as instances of noun phrase complementation. If we are willing to accept the cost of making the extraposition transformation obligatory for all verbs in the "believe" class, just in case the complementizer is "for-to," it becomes immediately clear that we not only have the transformational machinery sufficient to generate the sentence in (68) but also a ready explanation of the ungrammaticality of (62) and (63a). Let us consider this derivation in some detail.

(69) Sentence (68a)

First Cycle

I believe [[it]   [[John]   [have + en convince Bill]   ]   ]   BASE[10]
        N   NP   VP S NP

I believe [[it]   [[John]   [have convince + en Bill]   ]   ] T_{AUX}
        N   NP   VP S NP

Second Cycle

I believe [[it]   [for [John]   [to have convince + en Bill]   ]   ] T_{CP}
        N   NP   VP S NP

At this point, we require the obligatory application of the extraposition transformation. This transformation, applying vacuously with respect to the string in this instance, takes the complement sentence from under the domination of the NP which dominates it in the underlying structure.

I believe [[it]   ]   [for [John]   [to have convince + en Bill]   ] T_E
        N NP   NP   VP S

The pronoun replacement transformation (which has independent motivation in the subject complement system) is now defined and this string can be generated:

I believe [John]   [for [to have convince + en Bill]   ] T_{PR}
          NP   VP S

Finally, the obligatory complementizer deletion transformation applies.

I believe [John]   [[to have convince + en Bill]   ] T_{CD}
　　　　　NP　　　　　　　　　　　　　　　　　VP S

Post Cycle

I believe [John]   [[to have convinced Bill]   ]   M
　　　　　NP　　　　　　　　　　　　　　VP S

The derivation of (68b), which is generated from exactly the same underlying structure as (68a), differs from the derivation of (68a) only in that
the passive transformation applies on the first cycle of the former.

(70)   Sentence (68b)

First Cycle

I believe [[it]   [[John]   [have + en convince   [Bill]
　　　　　　N　　　　NP　　　　　　　　　　　　　　NP

[by + P]   ]   ]   ]   BASE
　　　MAN VP S NP

I believe [[it]   [[Bill]   [have + en be + en convince
　　　　　　N　　　　NP

[by + John]   ]   ]   ] T_P
　　　　MAN VP S NP

I believe [[it]   [[Bill]   [have be + en convince + en
　　　　　　N　　　　NP

[by + John]   ]   ]   ] T_{AUX}
　　　　MAN VP S NP

Second Cycle

I believe [[it]   [for [Bill]   [to have be + en convince + en
　　　　　　N　　　　　　NP

[by + John]   ]   ]   ] T_{CP}
　　　　MAN VP S NP

I believe [[it]   ]   [for [Bill]   [to have be + en convince + en
　　　　　　N NP　　　　　NP

[by + John]   ]   ] T_E
　　　　MAN VP S

I believe [Bill]   [for [to have be + en convince + en
　　　　　　NP

[by + John]   ]   ] T_{PR}
　　　　MAN VP S

I believe [Bill]   [[to have be + en convince + en
        NP

[by + John]   ]   ] T_{CD}
      MAN VP S

Post Cycle

I believe [Bill]   [[to have been convinced [by + John]   ]]   M
        NP   MAN VP S

We observed in an earlier discussion that the passive transformation
must apply before the extraposition transformation. Preserving this con-
straint with respect to sentence (61b), we note the following derivation.

(71)   Sentence (61b)

First Cycle

I believe [[it]   [[John]   [have + en convince Bill]]]   [by + P]   BASE
        N   NP   VP S NP   MAN

I believe [[it]   [[John]   [have convince + en Bill]]]   [by + P] T_{AUX}
        N   NP   VP S NP   MAN

Second Cycle

I believe [[it]   [for [John]   [to have convince + en Bill]]]
        N   NP   VP S NP

[by + P] T_{CP}
  MAN

[[it]   [for [John]   [to have convince + en Bill]]] be + en
 N   NP   VP S NP

believe [by + I] T_P
        MAN

[[it]   ] be + en believe [by + I]   [for [John]   [to have
 N NP   MAN   NP

convince + en Bill]   ] T_E
        VP S

[[it]   ] be believe + en [by + I]   [for [John]   [to have
 N NP   MAN   NP

convince + en Bill]   ] T_{AUX}
        VP S

[John] be believe + en [by + I]   [for [to have convince + en Bill]] T_{PR}
  NP   MAN   VP S

[John] be believe + en [by + I]   [[to have convince + en Bill]] T_{CD}
  NP   MAN   VP S

Post Cycle

[John] is believed [by + me]   [[to have convinced Bill]]   M
  NP   MAN   VP S

In addition to allowing us to explain the derivation of the sentences in (60) and (61) from a common underlying source through the application of an independently motivated transformation, namely, the pronoun replacement transformation, this analysis has another virtue. Consider the problem of the introductory "there" in true noun phrase complement constructions:

(72) a. everybody preferred (for) three chairs to be in the room

     b. it was preferred by everybody for three chairs to be in the room

     c. for three chairs to be in the room was preferred by everybody

     d. everybody preferred (for) there to be three chairs in the room

     e. it was preferred by everybody for there to be three chairs in the room

     f. for there to be three chairs in the room was preferred by everybody

Assuming the existence of a transformation that, in some appropriate fashion, converts a string of the form "three chairs are in the room" into "there are three chairs in the room," every sentence in (72) can be explained on the basis of the transformations proposed thus far in the present study. The introductory "there" takes subject position and is treated as the subject by all of the transformations applying in general to noun phrase complement constructions. Consider, however, the following sentences:

(73) a. everybody believes three chairs to be in the room

     b. three chairs are believed by everybody to be in the room

     c. everybody believes there to be three chairs in the room

     d. there is believed by everybody to be three chairs in the room

If we take the position that the sentences in (73) are instances of verb phrase complementation, we are forced to propose either a system in which the underlying object of the main verb can be a dummy or otherwise unspecified noun or that "there" is everywhere a possible expansion of NP. Making a long story short, we see immediately that the existence of the introductory "there" in sentences like (73) can be explained as an automatic consequence of the pronoun replacement transformation that, under the appropriate conditions, takes the subject of the complement sentence, no matter what that subject is, and substitutes it for the pronominal head.

It is of interest to observe the operation of the pronoun replacement rule when the depth of embeddings is increased. Consider, for example, the following sentence:

(74) I believe John's eating to be messy

(75)   Sentence (74)

First Cycle—no operations

I believe [[it]   [[[it]   [[John]   [eat]   ]   ]   [be messy]   ]   ]   BASE
   N N NP VP S NP   VP S NP

Second Cycle

I believe [[it]   [[[it]   [POSS [John]   [ing eat]   ]   ]
   N N   NP VP S NP

[be messy]   ]   ] T_{CP}
 VP S NP

Observe that extraposition cannot apply on this cycle since extraposition
is impossible for the "POSS-ing" complementizer.

I believe [[it]   [[[it]   [[John + POSS]   [eat + ing]   ]   ]
   N N   NP   VP S NP

[be messy]   ]   ] T_{AUX}
 VP S NP

I believe [[it]   [[[[John + POSS]   [eat + ing]   ]   ]   [be messy]   ]   ] T_{PD}
      NP   VP S NP   VP S NP

Third Cycle

I believe [[it]   [for [[[John + POSS]   [eat + ing]   ]   ]
   N   NP   VP S NP

[to be messy]   ]   ] T_{CP}
 VP S NP

I believe [[it]   ]   [for [[[John + POSS]   [eat + ing]   ]   ]
   N NP   NP   VP S NP

[to be messy]   ] T_E
 VP S

Notice that extraposition must have applied above since extraposition is
obligatorily defined on complements with "for-to" complementizers for
verbs of the "believe" class.

I believe [[[John + POSS]   [eat + ing]   ]   ]   [for [to be messy]   ] T_{PR}
    NP   VP S NP   VP S

I believe [[[John + POSS]   [eat + ing]   ]   ]   [[to be messy]   ] T_{CD}
    NP   VP S NP   VP S

Post Cycle

I believe [[[John's]   [eating]   ]   ]   [[to be messy]   ]   M
    NP VP S NP   VP S

A curious situation arises when the complementizer for the most deeply
embedded sentence is "that." By reconstructing the last derivation we

observe that if extraposition had applied on the second cycle we would have correctly generated a sentence like (76).

(76)   I believe it to be true that John is honest

If, on the other hand, the extraposition transformation had not applied on the second cycle, the grammar would have generated the quasi-grammatical sentence (77).

(77)   I believe that that John is honest is true

The status of (77) is not entirely clear, and one wonders if its strangeness might not be due to whatever produces the strangeness of multiple embeddings of various sorts. A similar strangeness is observed in sentences containing only the "that" complementizer.

(78)   a.   I believe that it is true that John is honest

        b.   I believe that that John is honest is true

In any event, the peculiarity of these sentences is not explained by the analysis being proposed here since both the sentences in (78) and those in (76) and (77) are generated as the consequence of the application of the same set of rules.

Another interesting fact about this analysis is that it makes it almost possible to eliminate the optional complementizer deletion transformation. Consider again the following pair of sentences:

(79)   a.   I hate for you to do these things

        b.   I hate you to do these things

We see that the preceding analysis affords an excellent explanation of the deletion of "for" in (79b). Let us suppose that the extraposition transformation applies vacuously (cf. pp. 41-42) to the noun phrase "it for you to do these things." The pronoun replacement transformation is now defined producing the string "you for to do these things." By the obligatory complementizer deletion transformation, this becomes "you to do these things." It thus seems possible to do away with the optional complementizer deletion transformation.

This proposal has two rather serious drawbacks. In the first place, it will be necessary to allow extraposition of complement sentences containing the "POSS-ing" complementizer since, otherwise, we shall still need an optional complementizer deletion transformation to handle the deletion of "POSS." But relaxing the restriction on extraposition, which may eventually be necessary to some extent, results in many of the ungrammatical sentences presented in the paradigm (30). A second drawback is equally as serious. Let us consider several examples of a verb for which complementizer deletion is obligatory, for example, "want."

(80)   a.   I want very much for John to go

    b.   I want John to go very much

    c.   *I want for John to go very much

    d.   *I want very much John to go

Our proposal neatly explains the grammaticality of (80a) and the ungrammaticality of (80d). Since the pronoun replacement transformation is blocked by the adverbial intervening between the pronominal head and the complement sentence, the subject of the complement sentence will not replace the pronominal head; consequently the "for" will not be contiguous with the VP and will not be deleted. But we observe that we can explain the nonoccurrence of (80c) only on the assumption that extraposition is obligatory for the verb "want." This, however, leaves us with no explanation of the grammaticality of (80b) since there is no indication whatever that extraposition has applied here. Thus we cannot rely on our proposal to explain all of the facts relating to complementizer deletion. It seems that the optional complementizer is still necessary.

But there is an interesting claim here nonetheless. The grammar tells us that sentences like (80b) may have two distinct derived constituent structures but one underlying structure. This follows from the fact that (80b) may have been derived either through the application of the complementizer deletion transformation on the one hand, or, on the other, through the vacuous application of the extraposition transformation and the subsequent application of the pronoun replacement and the obligatory complementizer deletion transformations. There is some recent psychological evidence supporting the plausibility of this circumstance.[11]

In closing the discussion of object complementation, it would not be beside the point to mention the several types of restrictions limiting the application the transformations involved in the complement system. These restrictions, which are idiosyncratic to particular verbs, will require description in the grammar; and the purpose of the following discussion is to identify some instances of this phenomenon. One of the more common restrictions has to do with the application of the optional complementizer transformation, as we have just seen. Consider the following pairs of sentences:

(81)   **a.**   1.   I would love for you to have it
              2.   I would love you to have it

        b.   1.   I can't bear for them to see me this way
              2.   I can't bear them to see me this way

        c.   1.   *I don't want for anybody to see me this way
              2.   I don't want anybody to see me this way

The foregoing considerations lead us to believe that this restriction can be explained by requiring the obligatory application of the optional complementizer deletion transformation for verbs like "want."

A second restriction has to do with the identity erasure transformation. We find instances where certain verbs taking object complement constructions require erasing and erased noun phrases to be identical. This restriction, which is also the property of all verb phrase complements, was not a property of the object complement constructions discussed earlier. Thus both of the sentences in (82) are grammatical.

(82) a.   I prefer for you to do it

     b.   I prefer to do it

But certain other verbs, such as "promise," do not have this freedom, a claim supported by the following data:

(83) a.   *I promise for you to bring money

     b.   I promise to bring money

Still other verbs, such as "require," "say," demand obligatory nonidentity of the erasing and erased noun phrases.

(84) a.   1.   I said for you to go
         2.   *I said (for me) to go[12]

     b.   1.   I require for you to have your hair cut
         2.   *I require (for me) to have my hair cut

At present, it is not clear how these restrictions are going to be stated in the grammar, although there seems little doubt that the system in which these restrictions are stated is not likely to be adequate if it does not handle identity restrictions in the same way for both verb phrase and noun phrase complementation.

The verb "promise" is unusual in still another respect. Sentences like (85) constitute a major exception to the erasure principle.[13]

(85)   I promised John to bring the money

The erasure principle predicts that the implicit subject of the complement sentence will be "John" rather than "I." It is quite doubtful that a principle that holds remarkably well for such a considerable number of cases will fail as the result of this one counterexample. The verb "promise" is peculiar in many respects; and there is every reason to interpret this result as advice to look more deeply into the analysis of this particular verb, for we are likely to find that the problem lies not with the erasure principle but with our analysis of the constructions in which this particular verb appears.

A final restriction concerns the application of the passive transformation to object complement constructions containing the "for-to" complementizer. Consider, for example, these data:

(86) a.   1.   a.   everybody loves John
            b.   John is loved by everybody

2.   a.   everybody loves for you to sing
      b.   *for you to sing is loved by everybody

b.   1.   a.   everybody dislikes John
         b.   John is disliked by everybody

    2.   a.   everybody dislikes for you to sing
         b.   *for you to sing is disliked by everybody

c.   1.   a.   everybody prefers John over Bill
         b.   John is preferred over Bill by everybody
    2.   a.   everybody prefers for you to sing
         b.   for you to sing is preferred by everybody

What these data demonstrate is that while passivization is possible in (86a, b) only if the object noun phrase does not dominate a complement sentence, passivization is possible for the verb "prefer" (86c) in either case. This fact suggests that although the passive transformation itself may not have been sensitive to the internal constituency of an NP, the restrictions on the application of this transformation which are idiosyncratic to particular verbs must be sensitive to the internal structure of NP's. At the present time, there are several mechanisms one might propose to state these idiosyncratic restrictions in the grammar, but there is no motivation for any other than that they may work. Until much more work can be done in this area, it is pointless to take up any more time in the discussion of what might be a correct formulation. There is simply too little evidence to establish any motivated system for handling these restrictions and, for purposes of the present study, this question is appropriately left open.

In still other cases, passivization is obligatory. Consider sentence (87).

(87)   John is said to be honest

In other cases, passivization is usually preferable

(88)   a.   John was rumored to be honest
      b.   John was alleged to be guilty

These sentences, analyzed as instances of noun phrase complementation similar to the analysis for the "believe" class of verbs discussed earlier, present no derivational difficulty. But it seems reasonably clear that the verbs in question will require some system of markers that advise of the obligatoriness of the passive transformation.

It is somehow ironic that the class of verbs that historically was the first to be investigated for the purpose of developing the analysis being presented here should turn out to be the most recalcitrant. The problem is that the criteria employed for differentiating verbs in terms of underlying structure seem to be inadequate at this point. The class of verbs includes "expect," "desire," and a few others. Consider the following paradigms:

(89)   a.   everybody expects (for) me to do what is right

    b.   it is expected by everybody for me to do what is right

    c.   what everybody expects is for me to do what is right

    d.   what is expected by everybody is for me to do what is right

(90) a.   everybody desired (for) me to be an honest man

      b.   it was desired by everybody for me to be an honest man

      c.   what everybody desired was for me to be an honest man

      d.   what was desired by everybody was for me to be an honest man

It seems beyond question that a noun phrase complement analysis must be assigned to the sentences in paradigms (89) and (90). Insofar as the sentences in (91) and (92) have the same interpretation as those in (89) and (90), we are led to believe that they follow the analysis for the verbs of the "believe" class, namely, that extraposition has applied to be followed by the pronoun replacement transformation and the obligatory complementizer deletion transformation.

(91) a.   I expect myself to do what is right

      b.   I am expected to do what is right

(92) a.   I desired myself to be an honest man

   ? b.   I was desired to be an honest man

But one wonders what to make of sentences like those in (93) and (94) which, in addition to requiring an object complement analysis, also have a prepositional phrase.

(93) a.   I expect (it) of myself that I will do what is right

      b.   I desire (it) of myself that I be an honest man

(94) a.   I expect it of myself to do what is right

      b.   I desire it of myself to be an honest man

These sentences present no derivation problem whatever. The problem is that there is a sense in which the sentences in (93) and (94) have the same semantic interpretation as those in (91) and (92). The open question is whether at this point the burden of explanation is to be placed on the semantic component or whether we should propose an analysis in which the sentences in (91) and (92) should be derived from the structures underlying those in (93) and (94). The considerations raised in the present study offer no way of resolving this question. In terms of these considerations, the sentences in (89), (90), (91), and (92) share a common underlying structure that differs from the structure underlying the sentences in (93) and (94). Progress in this area will no doubt depend upon distinctions far subtler than those which we were led to identify by the criteria for differentiating underlying structures proposed in this study.

4.2 Subject Complementation for Intransitive Verbs

The term <u>subject complementation</u> is a mnemonic referring to the instance of noun phrase complementation that arises through the expansion
of S into NP, VP. The application of phrase structure Rule 2 subsequently yields the string DET, N, S, VP, and it is to this configuration that the
discussion in the next few pages is devoted.

4.2.1. The "that" complementizer

The number of intransitive verbs in English taking subject complements
is comparatively small, but structures of this general type, the underlying structures of which are exemplified by the phrase structure diagram (95), raise questions of such importance that it will prove in-
structive to examine them in some detail.

(95)

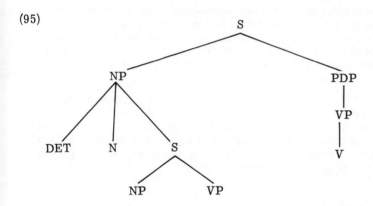

Representative sentences employing the complementizer "that" are the
following:

(96) a. it turns out that John is right

    b. it happened that John came early

The derivation of the sentences in (96) presents no difficulty that the
transformational apparatus outlined and discussed earlier cannot solve.
In particular, these sentences are generated simply as a function of the
application of the extraposition transformation to the underlying structure given in (95), as we see in the following derivation:

(97) Sentence (96b)

First Cycle—no operations

[[it] [[John] [came early]   ]   ] happened   BASE
  N   NP   VP   S NP

Second Cycle

[[it] [that [John] [came early]   ]   ] happened T_{CP}
 N   NP   VP S NP

[[it]   ] happened [that [John] [came early]   ] T_E
 N NP   NP   VP S

The one novel feature of the constructions in question is that the extraposition transformation appears to be obligatory since, as we see in (98),
the cognate sentences in which the extraposition transformation has not
applied are ungrammatical.

(98) a. *that John is right turns out

      b. *that John came early happened

Since it is not, in general, true that extraposition is always obligatory for
a noun phrase complement in sentence initial position, and we have noted
many such instances in the earlier discussion, it becomes necessary
apparently to postulate some instruction, probably incorporated into the
lexical entry for the appropriate verbs, which stipulates that the extraposition transformation must apply if the structural conditions for its
application are met. And in the case of constructions like (95), these conditions are always satisfied.

Although this verbal marker or instruction may be necessary, there are
certain considerations suggesting that it is not sufficient. In particular,
when verbs of the type under discussion are followed by a complement
sentence, the occurrence of a complement sentence containing a "that"
complementizer in subject position is completely appropriate and extraposition is not obligatory, as we see in (99).

(99) a. 1. that John is right turns out to be the case
          2. it turns out to be the case that John is right

      b. 1. that John came early happened to annoy Bill
          2. it happened to annoy Bill that John came early

The data in (99) suggest that the verbal marker regulating the application
of the extraposition transformation must be considerably more complex
than that originally envisioned. It must now consist of the assertion that
the extraposition transformation is obligatory just in case the verb is
followed by the sentence boundary "#." This additional complexity should,
perhaps, be taken as an indication that something is wrong with this
course of action. And, indeed, there are certain facts which this explanation does not account for.

The explanation of the optionality of the extraposition transformation that
is based upon the marker system crumbles under careful consideration
of the status of the complement sentence following the verb "happen," for
instance, in (99b). At first blush, we should consider the phrase "to annoy
Bill" as an instance of verb phrase complementation since it does not
participate in the variant constructions, such as the pseudocleft sentence,

which we have come to associate with noun phrase complement constructions. Thus, for example, neither of the following sentences constructed
on the assumption that the phrase "to annoy Bill" is a noun phrase complement is grammatical.

(100) a. *what that John came early happened was to annoy Bill

b. *what it happened was to annoy Bill that John came early

In the face of this evidence, we are inclined to believe that the phrase "to
annoy Bill" must, in actuality, be an instance of a verb phrase complement. But this alternate conclusion is not without serious difficulties
also, difficulties that become apparent upon careful consideration of other
instances of verb phrase complementation.

As a paradigm of intransitive verb phrase complementation, consider the
following sentence:

(101) the doctor condescended to examine John

As we should expect, if (101) is a correct paradigm, the pseudocleft sentence of (101) is impossible.

(102) *what the doctor condescended was to examine John

As an instance of verb phrase complementation, the sentence (101) has
roughly the underlying structure given in diagram (103).

(103)

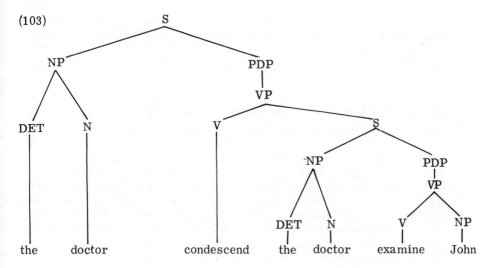

Let us suppose, now, that the grammar had generated "John" in the subject position of the main sentence instead of "the doctor." If the passive

transformation is subsequently applied to the complement sentence in
(103), this will allow for the derivation of the sentence (104).

(104) John condescended to be examined by the doctor

The sentences (101) and (104) have an entirely different meaning. This
difference is explained by the grammar by the fact that the two sentences
have different underlying structures. In the former, the noun phrase "the
doctor" is interpreted by the semantic component as the underlying subject of the main sentence. In the latter, the noun phrase "John" is so
interpreted. The fact that in (101) the complement sentence is active
while in (103) it is passive is of no consequence since both have the common underlying structure given in (103). It follows from this discussion
that a sentence S_1, derived from a structure like (103), will be synonymous with a sentence S_2 providing that, all other constituents being identical, the subject noun phrase of the main sentence is identical to the
subject noun phrase and the object noun phrase of the complement sentence. Examine the following sentences:

(105) a.   the doctor condescended to examine himself

      b.   the doctor condescended to be examined by himself

The semantic readings of all sentences based upon the structure in (103)
will be different unless these conditions are met. The difference in
meaning between sentences (101) and (104) exemplifies this conclusion.

Returning to the original question, namely, whether the phrase "to annoy Bill"
in (99b) is an instance of verb phrase complementation similar to (101),
we note a serious difficulty if we answer the question in the affirmative.
If the phrase "to annoy Bill" is an instance of intransitive verb phrase
complementation, then how can we explain the fact that sentences (99b. 1)
and (106) have the same meaning? (Sentence (99b. 1) is repeated here for
convenience.)

(99b. 1)   that John came early happened to annoy Bill

(106)   Bill happened to be annoyed that John came early

Since, in the verb phrase complementation analysis, the phrase "that
John came early" is the underlying subject of the main sentence in
(99b. 1) and since the noun phrase "Bill" is the underlying subject of the
main sentence in (106), the two sentences should be different in meaning.
But they are not. This fact may be taken to mean either that our formulation of intransitive verb phrase complementation is incorrect or, more
probably, that the phrase "to annoy Bill" in (99b) is simply not an instance of verb phrase complementation.

If the phrase "to annoy Bill" is neither an instance of noun phrase complementation nor an instance of verb phrase complementation, only one
possibility remains. This alternative asserts that the phrase "to annoy
Bill" does, in fact, originate as a noun phrase complement but that the
pronominal head of this construction no longer exists in a form to which

the pseudocleft sentence transformations can apply. Let us explore this possibility further.

Let us suppose that the underlying subject of the verb "happen" in (99b) is a noun phrase complement construction in which the subject of the complement sentence is itself a noun phrase complement construction. In other words, the underlying subject of the phrase "to annoy Bill" is "it that John came early" and that the entire complement sentence "it that John came early annoy Bill" is the subject of the verb "happen," the underlying structure being represented in (107).

(107) [[it]   [[[it]   [John came early]   ]   [annoy Bill]   ]   ] happen
　　　 N　　 N　　　　　　　　　　 S NP　　　　　　 VP S NP

Eschewing complementizer insertion for the time being, let us assume that on the second cycle, which concerns "it that John came early," the only applicable transformation is the pronoun deletion transformation, yielding a string like (108).

(108) [[it]   [[[John came early]   ]   [annoy Bill]   ]   ] happened
　　　 N　　　　　　　　　 S NP　　　　 VP S NP

On the third cycle, the extraposition transformation must apply (this rule being obligatory for verbs like "happen" as we have seen earlier), yielding the string (109).

(109) [[it]   ] happened [[[John came early]   ]   [annoy Bill]   ]
　　　 N NP　　　　　　　　　　　　 S NP　　　　　　 VP S

At this point, the pronoun replacement transformation, motivated in the discussion of object complementation, substitutes the noun phrase subject of the complement sentence for the pronominal head in the noun phrase which is the subject of "happen." The application of this transformation produces (110), that is, the string coinciding with (99b. 1). The complementizers are added here for the sake of clarity.

(110) [[that John came early]   ] happened [[to annoy Bill]   ]
　　　　　　　　　　　　 S NP　　　　　　　　　　 VP S

As we see in the formal derivation (115), if the extraposition transformation has been applied on the second cycle and if all subsequent transformations remain constant, we should have generated (111), the string coinciding with (99b. 2).

(111) [[it]   ] happened [[to annoy Bill]   [that John came early]   ]
　　　 N NP　　　　　　 VP　　　　　　　　　　 S S

This formulation has several advantages. In the first place, it allows for an explanation of the occurrence of the sentences in (96) and (99) and the nonoccurrence of the sentences in (98). The extraposition transformation is always obligatory. But complement constructions may end up in sentence initial position as the result of the pronoun replacement transformation. Second, this formulation explains the nonoccurrence of pseudocleft sentences in (100) as a function of this same transformation. Similarly, it explains another pseudocleft sentence phenomenon which we have not yet considered. Implicit in this analysis is the claim that the pronoun "it" in sentences (99a. 2, b. 2) is not the pronominal head of the entire underlying subject, that is, the first "it" in "it it that John came late annoy Bill." Rather, this analysis stipulates that the pronoun in the sentences is actually the pronominal head of the subject of the complement sentence "it that John came late annoy Bill." This prediction is confirmed by the fact that the pseudocleft sentence based upon the contrary assumption is ungrammatical (112).

(112)   *what happened was to annoy Bill that John came early

Only the pseudocleft sentence is possible, namely, the one based upon the pronominal head of the complement "that John came late."

(113) what happened to annoy Bill was that John came early

A third virtue of this analysis is that it offers an explanation of why subject complements containing the "POSS-ing" complementizer are impossible in (114a) but possible in (114b).

(114) a.   *John's coming early happened

     b.   John's coming early happened to annoy Bill

We can say that verbs like "happen" simply carry the restriction that the complement subject may not contain the "POSS-ing" complementizer. This restriction effectively blocks (114a) in our analysis but not (114b) since the complement containing the "POSS-ing" complementizer in this sentence is analyzed to be the subject of the verb "annoy," a verb that accepts "POSS-ing" complementizers in subject complements. The complement sentence "John's coming early" seems to be the subject only of "happened" in the underlying structure. As we have seen, this complement sentence attains the subject position only when the pronoun replacement transformation is applied.

For all of these reasons, the pronoun replacement transformation possesses great credibility and we may specify the derivations of the sentences under consideration in terms of this transformational rule (plus the obligatory complementizer deletion transformation which is a necessary consequence of this formulation) and others discussed previously. Clearly, the pronoun replacement transformation must follow the extraposition transformation in order of application since it is the latter that establishes an environment appropriate for the application of the former.

(115) Sentence (99b. 1)

First Cycle—no operations

[[it]   [[[it]   [John came late]   ]   [annoy Bill]   ]   ] happen   BASE
 N   N   S NP   VP S NP

Second Cycle

[[it] [[[it] [that John came late]   ]   [annoy Bill]   ]   ] happen T_{CP}
  N   N   S NP   VP S NP

[[it] [[[that John came late]   ]   [annoy Bill]   ]   ] happen T_{PD}
  N   S NP   VP S NP

Third Cycle

[[it] [for [[that John came late]   ]   [to annoy Bill]   ]   ] happen T_{CP}
  N   S NP   VP S NP

[[it]   ] happen [for [[that John came late]   ]   [to annoy Bill]   ] T_E
  N NP   S NP   VP S

[[that John came late]   ] happen [for [to annoy Bill]   ] T_{PR}
      S NP   VP S

[[that John came late]   ] happen [[to annoy Bill]   ] T_{CD}
      S NP   VP S

(116) Sentence (99b. 2)

First Cycle—no operations

[[it] [[[it] [John came late]   ]   [annoy Bill]   ]   ] happen   BASE
  N   N   V NP   VP S NP

Second Cycle

[[it] [[[it] [that John came late]   ]   [annoy Bill]   ]   ] happen T_{CP}
  N   N   S NP   VP S NP

[[it] [[[it]   ] [annoy Bill] [that John came late]   ]   ] happen T_E
  N   N NP   VP   S S NP

Third Cycle

[[it] [for [[it]   ] [to annoy Bill] [that John came late]   ]   ] happen T_{CP}
  N   N NP   VP   S S NP

[[it]   ] happen [for [[it]   ] [to annoy Bill] [that John came late]   ] T_E
  N NP   N NP   VP   S S

[[it]   ] happen [for [to annoy Bill] [that John came late]   ] T_{PR}
  N NP   VP   S S

[[it]   ] happen [[to annoy Bill] [that John came late]   ] T_{CD}
  N NP   VP   S S

4. 2. 2.   The "for-to" complementizer

Subject complement constructions containing the "for-to" complementizer present much the same type of problem with intransitive verbs as
do the subject complement constructions containing the "that" complementizer. Consider the following sentences:

(117) a.   1.   *for John to find gold happened

        2. *it happened for John to find gold
        3.   John happened to find gold

   b. 1. *for John to be unhappy appeared
        2. *it appeared for John to be unhappy
        3.   John appeared to be unhappy

The conclusion that sentence 3 in each group is, in fact, the result of the application of the pronoun replacement transformation and not an instance of verb phrase complementation follows from considerations identical to those raised in connection with the "that" complementizer earlier. We note, for example, that the "a" and "b" sentences of (118) are identical in meaning, a result opposite to that predicted by the hypothesis, which was that these sentences are instances of verb phrase complementation.

(118) a.   John happened to mention Bill

      b.   Bill happened to be mentioned by John

If we assume that the underlying structure of the sentences in (118) consists of the subject complement construction "it for John to mention Bill," then the synonymy of the sentences in (118) is an automatic consequence since these sentences differ only in their transformational derivation. More specifically, the passive transformation has been applied in the case of (118b) before the application of the identity erasure transformation, but the passive has not been applied in the case of (118a).

We observe, furthermore, that the fact that the pronoun replacement is obligatory explains the nonoccurrence of the pseudocleft sentence, for instance, in (119)

(119) a.   *what happened was for John to find gold

      b.   what happened was that John found gold

Since the pronoun replacement destroys the environment upon which the transformation deriving the pseudocleft sentence is defined, the derivation of (119a) is impossible.

In terms of this analysis, then, the derivation of sentence (117a. 3) proceeds as follows:

(120) Sentence (117a. 3)

First Cycle—no operations

[[it] [[John] [find gold]]] happened   BASE
  N   NP   VP S NP

Second Cycle

[[it] [for [John] [to find gold]]] happened T_{CP}
  N   NP   VP S NP

[[it]] happened [for [John] [to find gold]] T_E
  N NP   NP   VP S

[John] happened [for [to find gold]] T_{PR}
 NP   VP S

[John] happened [[to find gold]] T_{CD}
 NP   VP S

4.3   Subject Complementation for Transitive Verbs

Except for the nonapplication of the pronoun replacement transformation, subject complementation for transitive verbs does not differ from subject complementation for intransitive verbs. For this reason, the paradigm includes instances of subject complementation with all three complementizers. The derivation of these sentences is entirely a function of rules motivated in other parts of the complement system.

(121) a.   1.   that you came early surprised me
      2.   it surprised me that you came early

    b.   1.   for you to find me this way embarrasses me
      2.   it embarrasses me for you to find me this way

    c.   1.   John's playing the bugle annoys me
      2.   *it annoys me John's playing the bugle

(122) Sentence (121a. 1)

First Cycle—no operations

[[it] [you came early]] surprised me   BASE
 N   S NP

Second Cycle

[[it] [that you came early]   ] surprised me T_{CP}
 N   S NP

[[that you came early]] surprised me T_{CD}
      S NP

We observe that the extraposition transformation is not obligatory for subject complements if the main verb is transitive.

(123) Sentence (121a. 2)

First Cycle—no operations

[[it] [you came early]   ] surprised me   BASE
 N   S NP

Second Cycle

[[it] [that you came early]   ] surprised me T_{CP}
 N   S NP

[[it]   ] surprised me [that you came early] T_E
 N NP   S

(124) Sentence (121b. 1)

First Cycle—no operations

[[it] [[you] [find me this way]   ]   ] embarrasses me   BASE
 N   NP   VP S NP

Second Cycle

[[it] [for [you] [to find me this way]   ]   ] embarrasses me T_{CP}
 N   NP   VP S NP

[[for [you] [to find me this way]   ]   ] embarrasses me T_{PD}
      NP   VP S NP

(125) Sentence (121b. 2)

First Cycle—no operations

[[it] [[you] [find me this way]   ]   ] embarrasses me   BASE
 N   NP   VP S NP

Second Cycle

[[it] [for [you] [to find me this way]   ]   ] embarrasses me T_{CP}
 N   NP   VP S NP

[[it]   ] embarrasses me [for [you] [to find me this way]   ] T_{E}
 N NP   NP   VP S

(126) Sentence (121c. 1)

First Cycle—no operations

[[it] [[John] [play the bugle]   ]   ] annoys me   BASE
 N   NP   VP S NP

Second Cycle

[[it] [POSS [John] [ing play the bugle]   ]   ] annoys me T_{CP}
 N   NP   VP S NP

[[it] [[John + POSS] [play + ing the bugle]   ]   ] annoys me T_{AUX}
 N   NP   VP S NP

[[[John + POSS] [play + ing the bugle]   ]   ] annoys me T_{PD}
      NP   VP S NP

Post Cycle

[[[John's] [playing the bugle]   ]   ] annoys me   M
      NP   VP S NP

We observe that sentence (121c. 2) is impossible since the extraposition transformation is not defined on complements containing the "POSS-ing" complementizer. Thus, the pre-sentence pronoun deletion transformation must always apply, yielding sentences like (121c. 1).

4.4   Oblique Noun Phrase Complementation

4.4.1. Intransitive Oblique Noun Phrase Complementation

There are several instances of noun phrase complementation in English where the selectional restrictions on the complementizer of an object complement are in complementary distribution with the restrictions on oblique noun phrase complements. As an illustration, consider the following paradigm:

(127) a.   I decided that John shall represent us

      b.   *I decided on that John shall represent us

      c.   I decided for John to represent us

      d.   *I decided on for John to represent us

      e.   *I decided John's representing us

      f.   I decided on John's representing us

On the assumption that the verb "decide" has two analyses, one in which this verb takes a prepositional phrase and one in which it takes a direct object, one is forced to the unfortunate conclusion that not only does the lexical entry for "decide" contain two strict subclassificational features but the restrictions on the pronominal head of the complement construction as object of the verb are entirely distinct from the restrictions on the pronominal head in the prepositional phrase. In other words, the restrictions imposed upon the pronominal head as object must include the features $[+C][-D]$ and $[+C][+D][-E]$ where the first cluster represents the complementizer "that" and the second, the complementizer "for-to." The restrictions on the pronominal head when it appears in a prepositional phrase must include the features $[+C][+D]$ $[+E]$, the cluster representing the "POSS-ing" complementizer.

In the following pages, an attempt will be made to show that the lexical representation of such verbs as "decide" can be greatly simplified if it is assumed that the underlying structures for the grammatical sentences in (127) are identical. If it can be shown that the prepositional phrase analysis underlies all three cases, then it is no longer necessary to posit the complex array of restrictions just proposed.

The problems posed by the introduction of the preposition in the structure underlying the sentence (127f) are similar to those discussed in Chapter 3 in relation to the introduction of the complementizing morphemes. More specifically, we are confronted with an option: to introduce the preposition through the application of phrase structure rules or to introduce the preposition transformationally by a rule that is sensitive to the structure given in (128) and to the features on the verb that determine the particular preposition or set of prepositions appropriate to particular verbs.

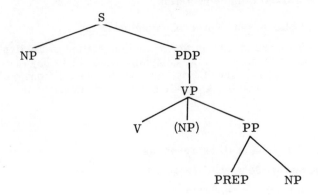

The issues that bear on the choice of a mechanism for introducing prepositions will not be discussed here since the way in which the prepositions are most adequately introduced into the phrase structure has little
if any effect on the general form of the rules employed in the description
of the predicate complement system.

Having introduced the constituent PREP into the structure underlying
sentence (127f), we observe that the transformations proposed earlier
are fully adequate to the task of generating the correct derived structure.

(129) Sentence (127f)

First Cycle—no operations

I decided [PREP [[it] [[John] [represent us]]]]   BASE
                       N   NP   VP S NP PP

Second Cycle

I decided [PREP [[it] [POSS [John] [ing represent us]]]] T_{CP}
                       N   NP   VP S NP PP

I decided [PREP [[it] [[John + POSS] [represent + ing
                       N   NP

us]]]] T_{AUX}
VP S NP PP

I decided [PREP [[[John + POSS] [represent + ing us]]]] T_{PD}
                            NP   VP S NP PP

Post Cycle

I decided [on   [[[John's] [representing us]]]]   M
                        NP   VP S NP PP

Considerations of simplicity determine that the complement constructions in the remaining grammatical sentences in paradigm (127) originate as noun phrase complements in prepositional phrases. If the claim
is made that all of the grammatical sentences in (127) have an underlying

prepositional phrase analysis, then, first, it is necessary to state for the verb "decide" only that it occurs before prepositional phrases (rather than before both prepositional phrases and noun phrases) and, second, it is totally unnecessary to specify any features of the pronominal head in the prepositional phrase except for the feature [+C] since all complementizer combinations are possible. Empirical justification arises when we examine the passive constructions and pseudocleft sentences related to the sentences in (127).

(130) a. 1. that John shall represent us was decided (on) by me
          2. what I decided (on) was that John shall represent us

      b. 1. for John to represent us was decided (on) by me
          2. what I decided (on) was for John to represent us

This analysis requires a preposition deletion rule deleting the preposition just in case it appears before a pronominal head marked either [+C][−D], the "that" complementizer, or [+C][−E], the "for-to" complementizer. This transformation is defined in Chapter 1 as the preposition deletion transformation T_{PPD}. Since the deletion of the preposition depends upon the contiguity of the preposition with the pronominal head, it follows that for the dialects in which the preposition is not deleted under passivization the preposition deletion rule must follow the application of the passive transformation. If the preposition deletion transformation precedes the passive transformation, then the preposition will invariably be deleted. The following data suggest, however, that such preposition deletion is rather uncommon.

(131) a. 1. they marveled that the plane flew at all
          2. that the plane flew at all was marveled at by them
          3. *that the plane flew at all was marveled by them

      b. 1. everyone rejoiced that you were happy
          2. that you were happy was rejoiced at by everybody
          3. *that you were happy was rejoiced by everybody

      c. 1. John insisted that you be here on time
          2. that you be here on time was insisted on by John
          3. *that you be here on time was insisted by John

Thus, preposition deletion must follow the passive transformation and must precede pronoun deletion. Furthermore, it is likely that the preposition deletion transformation must precede the pronoun replacement transformation and must follow the optional complementizer deletion transformation. In terms of these transformations, we can specify the derivation of sentence (127a) in the following fashion:

(132) Sentence (127a)

First Cycle—no operations

I decided [PREP [[it] [John shall represent us]   ]   ]   BASE
                       N   S NP PP

Second Cycle

I decided [PREP   [[it]   [that John shall represent us]   ]   ] T_{CP}
            N   S NP PP

I decided [[[it]   [that John shall represent us]   ]   ] T_{PPD}
           N   S NP PP

I decided [[[that John shall represent us]   ]   ] T_{PD}
                                     S NP PP

With the application of the passive transformation, we are able to derive sentences like (131c. 2)

(133) Sentence (131c. 2)

First Cycle—no operations

John insist [PREP   [[it]   [you be here on time]   ]   ]   [by + P]   BASE
                  N   S NP PP   MAN

Second Cycle

John insist [PREP   [[it]   [that you be here on time]   ]   ]   [by + P] T_{CP}
                  N   S NP PP   MAN

[[it]   [that you be here on time]   ]   be + en insist   [PREP]
 N   S NP   PP

[by + JOHN] T_P
    MAN

[[it]   [that you be here on time]   ]   be insist + en   [PREP]
 N   S NP   PP

[by + John] T_{AUX}
    MAN

[[that you be here on time]   ]   be insist + en   [PREP]   [by + John] T_{PD}
                     S NP   PP   MAN

Post Cycle

[[that you be here on time]   ]   was insisted   [on]   [by + John]   M
                     S NP   PP   MAN

An important consequence of the fact that the preposition deletion transformation follows the application of the passive transformation is that the same preposition deletion transformation accounts for the obligatory deletion of the agentive preposition "by." Consider the following examples:

(134) a.   1.   for you to see this mess embarrasses me
        2.   *I am embarrassed by for you to see this mess
        3.   I am embarrassed for you to see this mess

  b.   1.   to have you visit my home honors me

        2.   *I am honored by to have you visit my home

        3.   I am honored to have you visit my home

As is seen in the following derivation, sentences (134a. 2, b. 2) are effectively blocked by the obligatory application of the preposition deletion transformation.

(135) Sentence (134a)

First Cycle—no operations

[[it] [[you] [see this mess]]] embarrasses me [by + P]   BASE
 N   NP   VP S NP   MAN

Second Cycle

[[it] [for [you] [to see this mess]]] embarrasses
 N   NP   VP S NP

me [by + P] T_{CP}
    MAN

I be + en embarrass [by + [[it] [for [you] [to see this
                   N   NP

mess]]]] T_P
  VP S NP MAN

I be embarrass + en [by + [[it] [for [you] [to see this
                   N   NP

mess]]]] T_{AUX}
  VP S NP MAN

I be embarrass + en [[[it] [for [you] [to see this
                 N   NP

mess]]]] T_{PPD}
  VP S NP MAN

I be embarrass + en [[[for [you] [to see this mess]]]] T_{PD}
                 NP   VP S NP MAN

Post Cycle

I am embarrassed [[[for [you] [to see this mess]]]]   M
              NP   VP S NP MAN

This analysis provides a method for deciding on the derivational status of the morpheme "for" in places where there is no a priori reason to identify this morpheme as either the preposition "for" or the complementizer "for." Consider these sentences:

(136) a.   I hope for you to come on time

      b.   I hope that you will come on time

Superficially, the sentences appear to be instances of object complementation. A consideration of the pseudocleft sentences in (137) indicates, however, that a prepositional phrase analysis is, perhaps, more appropriate:

(137) a.   what I hope for is for you to come on time

b.   what I hope for is that you will come on time

Since we know from earlier considerations that the preposition deletion transformation is obligatory when the preposition precedes a pronominal head marked either $[+C][-D]$ or $[+C][-E]$, the conclusion necessarily follows that the "for" in the sentence (136a) is the complementizer "for." This morpheme could be a preposition only at the expense of making the preposition deletion rule less general, that is, by making it optional for verbs like "hope" when the complementizer is "for-to." Consider now the derivation of the sentence (136a) in terms of the analysis in which the preposition deletion transformation is obligatory:

(138) Sentence (136a)

First Cycle—no operations

I hope [PREP [[it] [[you] [come on time]]]]   BASE
$\qquad$ N $\quad$ NP $\qquad\qquad$ VP S NP PP

Second Cycle

I hope [PREP [[it] [for [you] [to come on time]]]] T_{CP}
$\qquad$ N $\qquad$ NP $\qquad\qquad$ VP S NP PP

I hope [[[it] [for [you] [to come on time]]]] T_{PPD}
$\qquad$ N $\qquad$ NP $\qquad\qquad$ VP S NP PP

I hope [[[for [you] [to come on time]]]] T_{PD}
$\qquad\qquad$ NP $\qquad\qquad$ VP S NP PP

Despite the fact that the optional complementizer deletion transformation is impossible for verbs like "hope," it is not, in general, impossible for prepositional phrase complement constructions, as we see in the following examples:

(139) a.   1.   I thought about the world's coming to an end
$\qquad$ 2.   I thought about the world coming to an end

b.   1.   I worried about the world's coming to an end
$\qquad$ 2.   I worried about the world coming to an end

Thus, the prepositional phrase noun phrase complements present optional complementizer deletion options in the same way as do object complement constructions.

There are many other prepositions that participate in constructions of the type under discussion. All of them seem to share the same properties as "on" and "for." Thus we shall not take the time to illustrate any of the derivations, but it is nonetheless clear that the rules proposed earlier are fully adequate to generate the following sentences as well as many others.

(140) a.   John persisted in reading
      b.   John persisted to read

(141) a.   I marveled at your being so late
      b.   I marveled that you were so late

(142) a.   I admit to being lazy
      b.   I admit that I am lazy

(143) a.   I boasted of being strong
      b.   I boasted that I was strong

4.4.2.   Transitive Oblique Noun Phrase Complementation

Once again, consideration of the pseudocleft sentences requires one to posit transitive oblique noun phrase complement constructions, that is, those where the phrase structure rules of Chapter 1 produce the configuration given in (144). Let us compare, for example, the two sentences in (145) with respect to this construction.

(144)

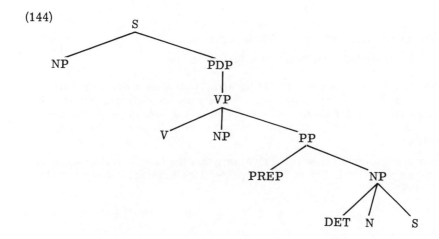

(145) a.   I reminded John to visit his ailing mother

      b.   I defied John to visit his ailing mother

(146) a.   what I reminded John of was to visit his ailing mother

      b.   *what I defied John (of) was to visit his ailing mother

The fact that the pseudocleft sentence is possible for (145a) and not (145b) suggests that underlying the former is a noun phrase complement construction. Furthermore, the occurrence of the preposition "of" in (146a) suggests that this noun phrase complement originates as the noun phrase of a prepositional phrase.

This analysis gains additional support from the occurrence of the "that" complementizer in sentences containing the verb "remind" but not in sentences containing the verb "defy."

(147) a. I reminded John that he should visit his ailing mother

　　　b. *I defied John that he should visit his ailing mother

We might reason that "defy" is a verb that simply does not allow the "that" complementizer, but this judgment would not help to explain the fact that the pseudocleft sentence is as possible for (147a) as it is for (145a), as we see in (148).

(148) what I reminded John of was that he should visit his ailing mother

Furthermore, if we adopt the position suggested by the facts, namely, that (145a) and (147a) are instances of preposition phrase complementation where the verb is transitive, it becomes possible to simplify the strict subcategorization information required by the verb. More specifically, sentences like (149) indicate that verbs like "remind," "convince," "persuade," and others may occur before a noun phrase object, which itself occurs before a prepositional phrase.

(149) a. I reminded John of the fact that he is late

　　　b. *I defied John of the fact that he is late

Assuming that sentences like (145a) and (147a) have a prepositional phrase in the underlying structure, we require no additional strict subcategorization information to be included in the lexical entry for the verb. In short, there is every advantage to be gained by making this assumption.

We observe in the following derivations that the transformational apparatus employed thus far is fully capable of generating sentences (145a) and (147a).

(150) Sentence (145a)

First Cycle—no operations

I reminded [John]　[PREP [[it]　[[John]　[visit his mother]　]　]　] BASE
　　　　　　NP　　　　　　N　　NP　　　　　　　　　VP S NP PP

Second Cycle

I reminded [John]　[PREP [[it]　[for [John]　[to visit
　　　　　　NP　　　　　　N　　　　NP

his mother]　]　]　]　　　　　　　　　　　　　　　　　　　T$_{CP}$
　　　　　VP S NP PP

I reminded [John] [PREP [[it] [for [to visit his mother]]]] T_{IE}
        NP   N   VP S NP PP

I reminded [John] [[[it] [for [to visit his mother]]]] T_{PPD}
        NP   N   VP S NP PP

I reminded [John] [[[for [to visit his mother]]]] T_{PD}
        NP   VP S NP PP

I reminded [John] [[[[to visit his mother]]]] T_{CD}
        NP   VP S NP PP

(151) Sentence (147a)

First Cycle—no operations

I reminded [John] [PREP [[it] [he should visit his mother]]]   BASE
        NP   N   S NP PP

Second Cycle

I reminded [John] [PREP [[it] [that he should visit
        NP   N

his mother]]] T_{CP}
 S NP PP

I reminded [John] [[[it] [that he should visit his mother]]] T_{PPD}
        NP   N   S NP PP

I reminded [John] [[[that he should visit his mother]]] T_{PD}
        NP   S NP PP

There are several constructions in English which in certain respects resemble those just discussed, but which also present a couple of curious problems. As an illustration, consider these sentences:

(152) a. I prevented the doctor from examining John

      b. I prevented John from being examined by the doctor

It will be observed immediately that sentences (152a) and (152b) have the same truth value synonymy, a fact which could not be explained on the assumption that the sentences in (152) are instances of transitive oblique noun phrase complementation as are the sentences (145a) and (149a). On this assumption, the underlying structures, and hence the semantic interpretation, of the sentences in (152) are different. In (152a), the underlying object of "prevent" is "the doctor," while in (152b), the underlying object is "John."

The second problem which arises with respect to (152) is that a transitive oblique noun phrase complement analysis predicts incorrectly the grammaticality of the pseudocleft sentences in (153).

(153). a. *what I prevented the doctor from was examining John

      b. *what I prevented John from was being examined by the doctor

Both of these problems can be resolved if it is assumed that the morpheme "from" in (152) is not an instance of PREP but a complementizer
of the basic form "from-ing." Consider the following derivation in terms
of this assumption:

(154) Sentence (152a)

First Cycle—no operations

I prevented [[it]   [[John] [go]   ]   ]   BASE
        N   NP   VP S NP

Second Cycle

I prevented [[it]   [from [John]   [ing go]   ]   ] T_{CP}
        N   NP   VP S NP

Since extraposition is blocked in the event the complementizer is "POSS-
ing" but not if the complementizer is "from-ing," extraposition can apply
to the string in the Second Cycle. It would appear, in fact, that extraposition is obligatory as it is for the "for-to" complementizers for the "believe" class of verbs.

I prevented [[it]   ]   [from [John]   [ing go]   ] T_E
        N NP   NP   VP S

I prevented [[it]   ]   [from [John]   [go + ing]   ] T_{AUX}
        N NP   NP   VP S

I prevented [John]   [from [go + ing]   ] T_{PR}
        NP   VP S

If we prevent the obligatory complementizer deletion transformation
from applying to the "from" complementizer, the grammar correctly
generates this string:

Post Cycle

I prevented [John]   [from [going]   ]   M
        NP   VP S

This analysis has several virtues that offset, perhaps, the cost of the
required restriction on the obligatory complementizer deletion transformation. First, the synonymy of the sentences in (152) is explained by the
fact that the two sentences do not differ in their underlying structures
except for the constituent marking the obligatory passive transformation
which does not affect the semantic interpretation. Second, the nonoccurrence of the pseudocleft sentences in (153) is explained in precisely the
same way as the nonoccurrence of such sentences in constructions containing main verbs of the "believe" class, that is, the application of pronoun
replacement transformation destroys the environment on which the

pseudocleft sentence transformations must be defined. Similarly, this analysis explains the introductory "there" phenomenon in sentences like (155).

(155) a.   Wyatt Earp prevented there from being trouble on the range

     b.   shelters will not prevent there from being great destruction

Finally, this analysis allows us to explain the synonymy of the sentences in (156) with those in (152).

(156) a.   I prevented the doctor's examining John

     b.   I prevented John's being examined by the doctor

In the sentences in (156) the complementizer is "POSS-ing" rather than "from-ing" but the underlying structures of the two pairs of sentences are identical in every respect. Their semantic interpretations, therefore, must be the same.

The introduction of a new complementizer, "from-ing," seems to be necessary as there is no other immediately apparent analysis that can account for so wide a range of facts with similar economy. But this conclusion raises a host of new questions concerning the status of other putative prepositions and concerning the adequacy of the descriptive apparatus proposed in this study in the light of whatever new complementizers might be discovered in following up this tentative analysis. These questions go far beyond the range of the present study. There is no independent justification at the present time for the complementizer "from-ing" other than that such a postulation accounts for the facts thus far investigated.

Notes

1.   It is unlikely that all of the paradigm sentences will be judged grammatical in a given dialect. These sentences simply illustrate the range of possible sentences based upon this complement construction which the author has observed in several dialects of English.

2.   For the sake of convenience, the pronominal head of a noun phrase complement construction $\begin{bmatrix} N \\ +PRO \end{bmatrix}$ will be represented as [it] in all subsequent derivations. Similarly, complementizers will be spelled out in the derivations rather than specified in terms of features. In the derivations beginning with (13), the abbreviation M stands for morphophonemic rules which will not be elaborated in this study.

3.   There are certain exceptions to this formulation. Consider sentences like the following:

    a.   I ask that John be allowed to come

    b.   *I ask John be allowed to come

It is perhaps not beside the point to note that verbs like "ask" belong to that small class of verbs which are exceptions to the erasure principle, as we see below.

    a.   I asked John to go

    b.   I asked of John to be allowed to go

That matter is discussed briefly later in Chapter 4.

4.   Cf. Noam Chomsky, "Current Issues in Linguistic Theory," in <u>The Structure of Language</u>, eds. J. A. Fodor and J. J. Katz (Englewood Cliffs, N.J.: Prentice-Hall, 1964).

5.   This follows from the fact the extraposition transformation is blocked in the event that the complementizer is "POSS-ing."

6.   The reader can readily test this assertion by comparing the number of complementizer features required by any three case formulations with the number required in the statement of the optional complementizer deletion transformation given in Chapter 1.

7.   This transformation would never apply in the event that structural indices 4 and 6 are not present. Furthermore, it could never be the case that both 4 and 6 would be present in the structural description.

8.   The remarks in note 1 of this chapter hold with respect to the "for-to" paradigm.

9.   In this instance the derived subject is the erased NP.

10.   The origin and interpretation of the "have" in this derivation will not be discussed, but it appears to be a reflection of the past tense required by this class of verbs with the "for-to" complementizer.

11.   Cf. T. Bever and Peter Rosenbaum, "The Psychological Verification of Linguistic Rules" (in preparation).

12.   Observe that the subject of this complement sentence can be deleted only when it is a pronoun like "someone."

13.   In addition, consider sentences like the following:

    a.   I demand of you to be allowed to come

    b.   I ask of you to be allowed to come

    c.   I request of you to be allowed to come

5. Verb Phrase Complementation

The reasons for postulating the existence of verb phrase complement constructions in English are the converse of those requiring the postulation of noun phrase complementation. Verb phrase complement constructions, generated by phrase structure Rule 1 in Chapter 1, require a derivational apparatus which makes use of the same set of transformations that we have seen to be necessary to the system of noun phrase complementation. In a sense, therefore, the next few pages constitute a review of the transformational machinery discussed thus far, for these rules apply to a different underlying structure. It is a measure of the adequacy of these rules that they generalize, as we shall see, to the more common verb phrase complement constructions of English.

5.1 Intransitive Verb Phrase Complementation

In proposing noun phrase complementation, we had reason to refer to pairs of sentences like the following:

(1)   a.   1.   Bill prefers to stay here
            2.   what Bill prefers is to stay here
            3.   to stay here is preferred by Bill
            4.   what is preferred by Bill is to stay here

       b.   1.   Bill condescended to stay here
            2.   *what Bill condescended was to stay here
            3.   *to stay here was condescended by Bill
            4.   *what was condescended by Bill was to stay here

We were able to explain the fact that all four of the sentences in (1a) are grammatical by assuming that the phrase "to stay here" was a noun phrase complement. On this assumption, passivization is perfectly appropriate since this phrase is dominated by an NP in the underlying structure. Furthermore, we can understand the grammaticality of the pseudocleft sentences of both the passive and active versions of this sentence on the assumption that the pseudocleft sentence transformations apply to instances of NP. In explaining the nonoccurrence of sentences (1b. 2, 3, 4), we can say either that the passive transformation and the pseudo-cleft sentence transformations do not apply for verbs such as "conde-scend," assuming a noun phrase complement analysis for (1b), or we can adopt the far more economical position that (1b) is simply not an in-stance of noun phrase complementation in the first place, in which case the nonapplication of the passive transformation and the pseudocleft sen-tence transformations follow necessarily. Taking the latter alternative, we were also able to demonstrate that the phrase "to stay here" must be an instance of verb phrase complementation, for to assume the contrary would make it difficult if not impossible to arrive at a reasonably simple formulation of the identity erasure transformation. In other words, we were able to show that the underlying structure for the sentence (1b) was roughly the following configuration.

(2)

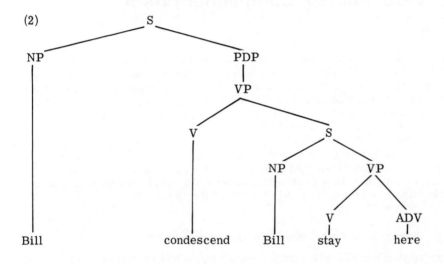

It is immediately apparent that the derivation of (1b. 1) from the under-lying structure (2) requires no rules in addition to those already moti-vated. The derivation can be specified in the following fashion.

(3)   Sentence (1b)

First Cycle—no operations

Bill condescended   [[Bill] [stay here]   ]   BASE
                        NP   VP S

Second Cycle

Bill condescended   [for [Bill] [to stay here]   ] T_{CP}
                          NP   VP S

Bill condescended   [for [to stay here]   ] T_{IE}
                              VP S

Bill condescended   [[to stay here]   ] T_{CD}
                          VP S

There is little more to say about the analysis of intransitive verb phrase complementation except to point out that the derivation of all verb phrase complement constructions depends upon the obligatory identity of the erasing and erased noun phrases, in this case the subject of the complement sentence and the subject of the main sentence. Thus, for example, sentences like (4) are impossible.

(4)   *I condescended Bill to go

We recall, however, that the identity of erasing and erased noun phrases is not always a necessary condition for the derivation of noun phrase complements, a fact attested by the sentences in (5).

(5)   a.   I hate for John to go

      b.   I hate to go

Indeed, in the system of noun phrase complements we even find cases where nonidentity seems to be a necessary condition for derivation.

(6)   a.   I said for John to go

      b.   I said (for someone) to go

      c.   *I said for me to go

The necessary identity of erasing and erased noun phrases also holds for certain fairly major classes of noun phrase complementation. For instance, there is no instance of a prepositional noun phrase complement for a transitive verb where identity of erasing and erased noun phrases is not a necessary condition for derivation. As an example, consider these sentences:

(7)   a.   1.   *I persuaded John for Bill to come
            2.   I persuaded John to come

      b.   1.   *I reminded John for Bill to visit his ailing mother
            2.   I reminded John to visit his ailing mother

There may well be an explanation for the necessary identity of erasing and erased noun phrases in the structures just presented, but this issue will not be taken up in the present study.

5. 2   Transitive Verb Phrase Complementation

On the basis of the rules already presented, the derivation of transitive verb phrase complement constructions is quite straightforward. We can establish the existence of such constructions by comparing the following sets of sentences:

(8) a. 1. somebody prefers for John to do the work
       2. what somebody prefers is for John to do the work
       3. for John to do the work is preferred
       4. what is preferred is for John to do the work

    b. 1. somebody trusts John to do the work
       2. *what somebody trusts is for John to do the work
       3. *for John to do the work is trusted
       4. *what is trusted is for John to do the work

Applying the same reasoning to the paradigm (8) as was just applied to paradigm (1), we arrive at the conclusion that sentence (8b. 1) is an instance of transitive verb phrase complementation having the underlying structure given in (9). The nonoccurrence of sentences (8b. 2, 3, 4) is thus predicted.

(9)

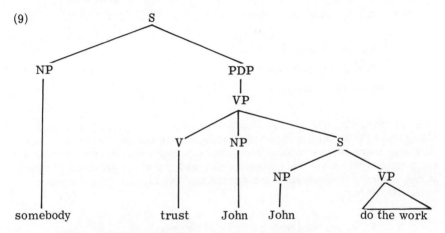

On the basis of the underlying structure (9), we can specify the derivation of (8b. 1) in the following fashion:

(10)   Sentence (8b. 1)

First Cycle—no operations

somebody trusts   [John] [[John] [do the work]   ]   BASE
                   NP   NP   VP S

Second Cycle

somebody trusts   [John] [for [John] [to do the work]   ] T_{CP}
                   NP   NP   VP S

somebody trusts   [John] [for [to do the work]   ] T_{IE}
                   NP   VP S

somebody trusts   [John] [[to do the work]   ] T_{CD}
                   NP   VP S

This derivational procedure is common to all verb phrase complement constructions. There is certain additional apparatus required to handle those cases in which the complementizer "to" is either obligatorily or optionally deleted, as in (11), but the details of this operation are sufficiently transparent so that it is probably unnecessary to go into further detail on this phenomenon.

(11) a. 1. I helped John to build the house
         2. I helped John build the house

      b. I let John go

      c. I made John go

It seems reasonably clear that the "to" deletion transformation will have to be dependent upon some sort of verbal marker since the deletion of the "to" is an idiosyncratic property of an extremely small number of verbs.

5.3 Oblique Verb Phrase Complementation

The necessity of positing underlying structures of this type follows from a consideration of paradigm (12).

(12) a. 1. they prevailed upon John to represent us[1]
         2. what they prevailed upon John for was to represent us

      b. 1. they hit upon John to represent us
         2. *what they hit upon John for was to represent us

These data suggest a derivation for sentence (12b.1) that follows the pattern set by the derivations of the verb phrase complement constructions in the preceding two sections.

(13) Sentence (12b.1)

First Cycle

they hit [PREP John] [[John] [represent us]]   BASE
                PP   NP   VP S

Second Cycle

they hit [PREP John] [for [John] [to represent us]] T_{CP}
                PP   VP S

they hit [PREP John] [for [to represent us]] T_{IE}
                PP   VP S

they hit [PREP John] [[to represent us]] T_{CD}
                PP   VP S

Post Cycle

they hit [upon John] [[to represent us]]   M
                PP   VP S

5.4   Special Problems

The class of verbs that includes such items as "taste," "smell," "feel," and others seems to require certain additional apparatus.[2] Consider these sentences:

(13)   a.   the meat tastes salty to me

      b.   the milk smells good to me

      c.   the batter feels lumpy to me

We observe, however, that such sentences as those in (14) have an entirely different status from those in (13).

(14)   a.   *the meat tastes salty to the tree

      b.   *the milk smells good to the pencil

      c.   *the batter feels lumpy to the spoon

The restrictions which are imposed upon the noun phrase in the prepositional phrases in (13) and (14) we observe to be identical to those imposed upon the subjects of the following sentences:

(15)   a.   1.   I taste the meat
          2.   I smell the milk
          3.   I feel the batter

      b.   1.   *the tree tastes the meat
          2.   *the pencil smells the milk
          3.   *the spoon feels the batter

The statement of the restrictions noted in (15) can be generalized, that is, stated only once in the grammar, if we assume that the sentences in (13) are derived from sentences in which the noun phrase observed in the prepositional phrases of (13) originate as the underlying subjects of these sentences. In other words, we propose that the sentences in (13) are actually instances of verb phrase complementation and that, in the course of the derivation, the subject and object of the main sentence are inverted. We may specify this derivation in the following fashion:

(16)   Sentence (13a)

First Cycle—no operations

I taste [the meat] [[the meat] [be salty]   ]   BASE
         NP   NP   VP S

Second Cycle

I taste [the meat] [for [the meat] [to be salty]   ] T_{CP}
                    NP   VP S

I taste [the meat] [for [to be salty]   ] T_{IE}
                  VP S

The identity erasure transformation must precede the subject-object inversion transformation. Otherwise, the erasure principle will fail.

[the meat] taste [for [to be salty]   ] to + me   T$_{SOI}$
  NP   VP S

The passive transformation must follow the subject-object inversion
transformation since if it does not, the grammar generates sentences
like "the meat was tasted by me to be salty." Note furthermore that
since the subject-object inversion transformation places the subject
noun phrase to the right of the verb phrase complement sentence, the
nonapplication of the passive transformation directly follows.

[the meat] taste [[to be salty]   ] to + me   T$_{CD}$
  NP   VP S

[the meat] taste [[salty]   ] to + me   T$_{TB}$
  NP   VP S

The transformation T$_{TB}$ which was not defined in Chapter 1 plays a role
in a variety of complement constructions. Thus one finds sentences like
"I consider John to be a fool" and "I consider John a fool."

Post Cycle

[the meat] tastes [[salty]   ] to + me   M
  NP   VP S

The subject-object inversion transformation is not without its difficulties
but it does appear to be a tentative approximation of a rule clearly
necessary in some form. It is not inconceivable that a rule of this general type will have an important extension in the analysis that attempts
to relate the sentences in the following pairs:

(17) a. 1. I value the book
          2. the book is valuable to me

      b. 1. I benefit from your kindness
          2. your kindness is beneficial to me

But the development of strong motivation for formulating a general subject-object inversion transformation is not within the scope of the present work, and the employment of this rule to handle cases like those in
(13)-(16) is to be taken more as a suggestion than as a rule.

Notes

1. We observe that (12a) is actually an instance of oblique noun
    phrase complementation since there is no other analysis which
    could explain the occurrence of the preposition "for" in the pseu-
    docleft sentence (12a.2).

2. This problem was suggested to the author by Paul Postal.

6. Complementation in Adjectival Predicate Constructions

The behavior of predicate complement constructions in adjectival structures is, in many ways, remarkably similar to the behavior of these
same constructions in the verbal structures discussed in earlier chapters. Certain of these adjectival constructions will be given brief consideration in this chapter. The analyses provided should be taken more
as suggestions than as definitive since it will become immediately clear
that a fairly wide range of phenomena have not been taken into consideration. For instance, there is little doubt that a more insightful analysis
will reveal many instances where adjectival complement constructions
are probably to be considered as derivationally related to cognate verbal
complement constructions. The purpose of the brief exposition in this
chapter is simply to show that many of the transformations discussed
earlier are equally applicable in cases where the predicate of the sentence is, in its derived structure at least, an adjective.

6.1 Oblique Noun Phrase Complementation

A great many adjectives take prepositional phrases containing a noun
phrase complement construction. Although very few adjectives participate in a complete paradigm, allowing for all three complementizer possibilities in the complement sentence, one finds "scared" in this class of
adjectives. Consider the following paradigm:

(1) a. I am scared of leaving home at this time

     b. I am scared that I will not be able to do the work

     c. I am scared to find out the truth.

Evidence supporting the position that the "b" and "c" sentences in the
paradigm are instances of prepositional noun phrase complementation

as well as the "a" sentence is observed in the fact that the pseudocleft sentences relating to the sentences in the paradigm are grammatical.

(2) a.   what I am scared of is leaving home at this time

b.   what I am scared of is that I will not be able to do the work

c.   what I am scared of is to find out the truth

That the sentences in the paradigm bear an obvious relation to the verbal sentences in (3) does not remove the necessity of positing structures of this type since, as the pairs in (4) attest, there is no immediately apparent verbal counterpart to the great majority of adjectives in this class.

(3) a.   leaving home at this time scares me

b.   it scares me that I will not be able to do the work

c.   it scares me to find out the truth

(4) a.   1.   I was aghast at John's hitting Bill
      2.   I was aghast that John hit Bill

b.   1.   I am aware of John's having left
      2.   I am aware that John left

The derivation of the sentences in this paradigm is perfectly straightforward and, as we see in the following illustration, includes only the transformational machinery requisite to the derivation of predicate complement constructions in verbal sentences.

(5)   Sentence (4b. 1)

First Cycle—no operations

I am aware [PREP [[it] [[John] [have left]]]]   BASE
                        N   NP   VP S NP PP

Second Cycle

I am aware [PREP [[it] [POSS [John] [ing have left]]]] T_{CP}
                        N   NP   VP S NP PP

I am aware [PREP [[it] [[John + POSS] [have + ing left]]]] T_{AUX}
                        N   NP   VP S NP PP

I am aware [PREP [[[John + POSS] [have + ing left]]]] T_{PD}
                          NP   VP S NP PP

Post Cycle

I am aware [of [[[John's] [having left]]]]   M
                      NP   VP S NP PP

(6)   Sentence (4b. 2)

First Cycle—no operations

I am aware [PREP [[it] [[John] [left]]]]   BASE
                      N   NP   VP S NP PP

Second Cycle

I am aware [PREP [[it] [that [John] [left]]]]   T$_{CP}$
                      N   NP   VP S NP PP

I am aware [[[it] [that [John] [left]]]]   T$_{PPD}$
                   N   NP   VP S NP PP

I am aware [[[that [John] [left]]]]   T$_{PD}$
                         NP   VP S NP PP

Paralleling verbs like "hope," which require the preposition "for" in the
underlying structure, one finds adjectives like "eager," "anxious,"
"ready," and several others. Consider, for example, the following sentences:

(7)   a.   I am eager for John to get going

       b.   I am anxious for you to see my etchings

       c.   I am getting ready to take the examination

The data provided by the pseudocleft sentence constructions once again
require one to postulate an underlying preposition phrase analysis.

(8)   a.   what I am eager for is for John to get going

       b.   what I am anxious for is for you to see my etchings

       c.   what I am getting ready for is to take the examination

There are a great many other adjectives which take prepositional noun
phrase complements with prepositions other than those mentioned, but
they present sufficiently few additional difficulties that further study is
not necessary at this time.

6. 2   Subject Complementation

Subject noun phrase complementation is as productive a process in adjectival constructions as it is in verbal construction. Consider the sentences in the following paradigm:

(9)   a.   1.   that John decided to fight is admirable
              2.   that he wants to do it is reasonable
              3.   that nothing works here is peculiar

       b.   1.   for him to want to go is admirable
              2.   for you to wish to make money is reasonable
              3.   for him to say that was peculiar

       c.   1.   John's being prompt is admirable
              2.   his wanting to go is reasonable
              3.   its being so cold in here is peculiar

There are two bits of evidence supporting the view that the sentences in (9) constitute instances of noun phrase complementation. First, we observe that extraposition is possible when the complementizer is either "that" or "for-to." Extraposition, as we have seen much earlier, depends upon the contiguity of the constituent S with the pronominal head of the complement construction.

(10)   a.   1.   it is admirable that John decided to fight
            2.   it is reasonable that he wants to do it
            3.   it is peculiar that nothing works here

       b.   1.   it is admirable for him to want to go
            2.   it is reasonable for you to wish to make money
            3.   it was peculiar for him to say that

Second, the pseudocleft sentence construction is possible for all sentences in paradigm (9).

(11)   a.   what is admirable is that John decided to fight

       b.   what is reasonable is for you to wish to make money

       c.   what is peculiar is his wanting to go

The derivations of the sentences (9)-(10) parallel the derivations proposed for subject complementation in verbal constructions, and there seems little reason to go through these derivations here.

Interestingly enough there are several adjectives such as "likely" which parallel verbs like "happen" in requiring, at least in the case of the "for-to" complementizer, obligatory extraposition and pronoun replacement. Consider, for example, the following series of sentences.[1]

(12)   a.   we are likely to be ready on time

       b.   *for us to be ready is likely

       c.   *it is likely for us to be ready

We could explain the grammaticality of (12a) in terms of a verb phrase complement analysis, but in doing this we should, first, lose in economy and, second, fail to explain certain semantic facts. Concerning the first point, it is clearly more expensive to assign distinct analyses to adjectives such as "likely," a subject complement analysis for cases like (13), and a verb phrase complement analysis to handle (12a).

(13)   a.   that we will be ready on time is likely

       b.   it is likely that we will be ready on time

Second, if we assume a verb phrase complement analysis for (12a), we fail to explain the truth value synonymy of the two sentences in (14).

(14)   a.   the egg is likely to be broken by John

       b.   John is likely to break the egg

If, on the other hand, we assume a subject complement analysis, this synonymy is explained automatically since the two sentences differ only in the application of the passive transformation to a common underlying structure in the case of (14a). Thus, the derivation of the sentence (14a) might be as follows:

(15)   Sentence (14a)

First Cycle

[[it] [[John] [break the egg [by + P]   ]   ]   ] be likely   BASE
 N   NP   MAN VP S NP

[[it] [[the egg] [be + en break [by + John]   ]   ]   ] be likely T_P
 N   NP   MAN VP S NP

[[it] [[the egg] [be break + en [by + John]   ]   ]   ] be likely T_{AUX}
 N   NP   MAN VP S NP

Second Cycle

[[it] [for [the egg] [to be break + en [by + John]   ]   ]   ] be
 N   NP   MAN VP   S   NP

likely T_{CP}

[[it]   ] be likely [for [the egg] [to be break + en [by +
 N NP   NP

John]   ]   ] T_E
 MAN VP   S

[the egg] be likely [for [to be break + en [by + John]   ]   ] T_{PR}
 NP   MAN   VP   S

[the egg] be likely [[to be break + en [by + John]   ]   ] T_{CD}
 NP   MAN   VP   S

Post Cycle

[the egg] is likely [to be broken [by + John]   ]   ]   M
 NP   MAN   VP   S

In terms of certain other subject complement constructions the generality of the pronoun replacement once again becomes an issue. Consider these sentences:

(16)   a.   for John to go is important

     b.   it is important for John to go

     c.   *John is important to go

(17)   a.   for you to see a doctor would be worthwhile

     b.   it would be worthwhile for you to see a doctor

     c.   *you would be worthwhile to see a doctor

We have two ways of explaining the nonoccurrence of the "c" sentences in (16) and (17). We might say, simply, that these particular adjectives do not undergo the pronoun replacement transformation and establish an appropriate system of verbal markers accordingly. There is a second possibility which is slightly more appealing because of its greater generality. We observe that it is just the adjectives in question that apparently allow a prepositional phrase following the adjective in the underlying structure.

(18)   a.   1.   it is important (to somebody) for John to go
              2.   it is important to John to go

        b.   1.   it would be worthwhile for the doctor for you to see him
              2.   it would be worthwhile for you (for you) to see the doctor
              3.   to see the doctor would be worthwhile for you

These data suggest the possibility of explaining the nonoccurrence of the "c" sentences in terms of the order of the deletion of the prepositional phrase. Although the details of this deletion go beyond the scope of the present study, it is a strong possibility that the pronoun replacement transformation may precede whatever transformation deletes the prepositional phrase, in which case the former is automatically blocked. Even though the prepositional phrase deletion rules may subsequently apply, the pronoun replacement transformation no longer can.

6.3   Verb Phrase Complementation

There are several adjectival complement constructions that, on the basis of the criteria discussed in this study, seem to call for a verb phrase complement analysis. Consider the following sentences:

(19)   a.   1.   John was happy to leave early
              2.   *what John was happy (PREP) was to leave early

        b.   1.   John was unable to see things clearly
              2.   *what John was unable was to see things clearly

        c.   1.   you are welcome to come
              2.   *what you are welcome is to come

The nonoccurrence of the cleft sentences does not prove, however, that these adjectival constructions do not belong to the same class as those discussed with respect to the adjective "likely." In other words, the pseudocleft sentence might be obviated by the application of the pronoun replacement transformation. But this possibility is negated because, as we observe in (20), the sentences in each pair do not have the same truth value synonymy, a fact that is explained by assuming distinct underlying structures.

(20)   a.   1.   the doctor was happy to examine John
              2.   John was happy to be examined by the doctor

        b.   1.   the nurse was unable to attend to John today
               2.   John was unable to be attended to by the nurse today

We thus conclude that the grammatical sentences in (19) are instances of verb phrase complementation and to be derived in exactly the same manner as the intransitive verb phrase complement construction discussed in Chapter 5.

6.4   Special Problems

One of the most recalcitrant problems in the predicate complement system concerns the extremely productive class of adjectives that includes items as "clever," "wise," "honorable," and at least a couple of hundred others. The specific problem concerns the relatedness of the sentences in (21) with sentence (22).

(21)   a.   to leave early was wise of John

       b.   it was wise of John to leave early

(22)   John was wise to leave early

Certain possibilities suggest themselves, but, as we shall see, none of them are without difficulties.

One of the more interesting analyses makes use of the pronoun replacement transformation. What makes the use of this transformation possible is the curious set of identity erasure options existing for this class of adjectives. More specifically, we observe the following possibilities:

(23)   a.   it was wise of John for him to leave early

       b.   it was wise of John to leave early

       c.   it was wise for John to leave early

In other words, we apparently have the option of deleting either the "erasing" noun phrase in the main sentence or the "erased" subject noun phrase in the complement sentence. This property is common to another class of adjectives, the class containing adjectives like "difficult," as in (24).

(24)   a.   it was difficult for John for him to pass the exam

       b.   for John to pass the exam was difficult

       c.   to pass the exam was difficult for John

Returning to the sentences in (23), we observe that if the option of deleting the connected noun phrase in the main sentence is taken, the pronoun replacement transformation is defined (on the string "it was wise [for John to leave early]") and we may generate sentence (22) accordingly.

A second possibility, although one which is beset by difficulties more severe than simply a lack of knowledge concerning the rules governing connection erasure options, attempts to relate (22) and perhaps the sentences in (21) to the following sentence:

(25)   John was wise in leaving early

To generate (22) on the basis of the structure underlying sentence (25) requires us to posit that (22) is an instance of prepositional complementation. In this view, the only difference between (22) and (25) is that the complement sentence in the former contains the "for-to" complementizer while the latter contains the "POSS-ing" complementizer. Several unfor-

tunate findings ensue from a careful study of this analysis. First, we find
that the noun phrase complement construction proposed here is the first
in this entire study for which the pseudocleft sentence is impossible, as
we see in (26). One is naturally reluctant to give up what has proved to
be such a powerful generalization.

(26) *what John was wise in was to leave early

If we make a deeper claim and assert that the prepositional phrase structure in (25) underlies (21) and (22) and that an inversion rule similar to
that discussed in Chapter 5 establishes a structure from which the sentences in (21) and (22) are subsequently derived by the transformational
apparatus already motivated, we can perhaps explain the nonoccurrence
of (26). But this involves us in other messy problems, such as explaining
why this inversion rule is obligatory if the complementizer is "for-to"
and optional otherwise and how it happens that the preposition "in" is
necessarily deleted so as to generate (27a) and not (27b).

(27) a.   leaving early was wise of John

      b.   *leaving early was wise of John in

In short, the considerations raised in the present study do not offer a way
of relating the sentences in (21) and (25). Such a proposal seems to raise
more problems than it solves. Furthermore, the derivation of (22) seems
to be more appropriately handled in terms of the structure underlying the
sentences in (21) than in terms of the structure underlying (25). It is
quite possible that a broader study of these phenomena will yield an insightful analysis in which the constraints governing the classification of
complement constructions suggested in this study will prove to be arti-
ficial. And it is no doubt with respect to the adjectives under discussion
that future research may be expected to yield more informative results.

The last construction deserving mention is a class of adjectives that
includes "difficult" and "easy." These adjectives demand the formulation
of an entirely new transformation, one which takes the final noun phrase
in the verb phrase of the complement sentence and substitutes it for the
pronominal head after the application of the extraposition transformation.
Consider the following sentences:

(28) a.   for John to hit Bill is difficult

      b.   it is difficult for John to hit Bill

      c.   Bill is difficult for John to hit

The transformation required to generate sentence (28c), which probably
depends upon the prior application of whatever rule deletes the erasing
NP in the derivation of sentences like (22), has roughly the following form.

(29)   W [[it]   ] AUX ADJ [[+C] NP AUX [V (PREP) NP] X] Y
            N NP   VP S
       1   2   3   4   5   6   7   8   9   10 11 12

       ⟹ 1, 10, 3, 4, 5, 6, 7, 8, 9, Ø, 11, 12

This summary of predicate complementation in adjectival structures is by no means complete. The reason for the brief discussion is to show that, with respect to predicate complementation, verbal and adjectival constructions share many properties in common. It would not speak well for the rules proposed in this study if they cannot be generalized to predicate complementation in both verbal and adjectival constructions. It may be that the general adequacy of the rules for adjectival complementation is more a function of the incompleteness of the present study of adjectival complementation than it is a true reflection of the near symmetry of the systems of verbal and adjectival complementation. More substantial study of adjectival complementation is required before the two systems can be rigorously compared. The most conservative assertion, namely, that the rules required to handle predicate complementation in verbal constructions also handle many cases of predicate complementation in adjectival constructions, is probably the strongest claim that can be made at the present time.

Notes

1.   Certain liberties are being taken in the assumption that words such as "likely," "sure," and "certain" are adjectives. There are grounds for arguing that these items are somewhat peculiar adverbs. This fact is not overly consequential should it turn out that lexical items must be marked in some fashion for the application of the pronoun replacement transformation. The present study suggests certain ways of avoiding having to mark lexical items for the application of pronoun replacement, e.g. ordering of prepositional phrase deletion and pronoun replacement. We should not be surprised, however, if subsequent research shows that lexical markers for pronoun replacement are absolutely necessary.

7. A Historical Perspective

The most provocative work on the predicate complement constructions
of English falls into two major categories: the so-called traditional
approach, best charaterized by the work of Poutsma and Jesperson, and
the generative transformational approach including primarily the work
of Chomsky, Lees, and Fillmore. The traditional view of complementation is based upon descriptive methodology underlying which is the goal
of explicating the structure of sentences in English in terms of the re-
lationship between words and an abstract logical structure implicit in
every grammatical English sentence. Perhaps it is true, as Lees suggests,[1] that the traditional approach to language study differs from the
transformational approach only to the extent that the scholars involved
in traditional linguistics did not have access to the formal apparatus
allowing the recursive specification of the well-formed sentences in a
natural language. But it is indeed a moot point whether the mere availa-
bility of such techniques would have been sufficient to insure that the
traditionalists would come to view explanation rather than simply description as the primary goal of linguistic inquiry. Whatever else a traditional grammar may contain, the deficiencies of the traditional
approach can be traced ultimately to the fact that the goal of linguistic
inquiry was, for the traditionalists, not a matter of justification but a
matter of description.

Our interest in the traditional approach to the problem of complementation stems from the fact that the traditional grammarians considered
it important for a linguistic description to take cognizance of a fairly
wide range of introspective linguistic data, in particular, judgments
about relations between words in sentences, about the identification of
parts of speech and the role played by the parts of speech in sentences,
about the constituency of sentences as these constituents fulfill the logical conditions imposed upon sentences, and so forth. The art consisted
not in providing a framework in which these human intellectual abilities
might be explained but in simply observing how various arrangements of
words contribute to the meaning of sentences. To take a specific
example, both Poutsma and Jespersen acknowledge that though an infini-

tive clause may express an action or state, the person or thing with which the action or state is associated is usually not indicated in any way in the infinitive clause. For both grammarians it was sufficient simply to indicate the deletion. The specification of which word or clause in the "head-sentence," to use Poutsma's term for the main sentence, is the same as the deleted word of the clause in the complement sentence was never considered an issue. Thus, it is of interest that the implicit subject of the complement sentence in "John promised to go" is the subject of the head-sentence while the implicit subject of the complement sentence in "we defy you to go" is the object of the head-sentence. In other words, subject deletion in "for-to" and "POSS-ing" complements was, in the traditional view, an important fact but not a fact that required explanation.

The central concern of a traditional approach to complementation is perhaps best understood in terms of the traditionalists' views on the constituency of sentences. Assuming that well-formed sentences in a language consist of two levels of constituents, logical and grammatical, the traditional grammarians sought to "discover" grammatical constituents on the basis of intuitions about logical constituents. Logical constituency refers to a definition of the sentence according to which it is said to consist minimally of a subject and a predicate. A predicate may consist of a verb and its object. Furthermore, subjects, objects, and verbs (where no distinction is drawn between the logical status of a verb and its grammatical status) may be modified by additional constituents variously referred to as adjuncts, modifiers, and occasionally, complements. A grammatical analysis consists first in showing the constituency of these logical categories and second in deriving a classification of the various parts of speech and larger grammatical units that operate as logical constituents.

This methodology leads to some very interesting results. In the first place, Poutsma observes a strong functional similarity between subordinate clauses with "that" and infinitive and gerundive clauses. In particular, he notes that all three clauses may appear as the subject of a verb. Similarly, they may appear as the object of a verb. Since all three constructions have the same logical constituency, he reasonably assumes that they share a common feature in the language. This observation, correct though it may be, left Poutsma with a conceptual problem that his grammatical system did not allow him to solve, namely, there was no way in which he could express the notion "common feature." Insofar as notions like "subject," "object," and so forth are logical structures expressing merely the relation between words in well-formed sentences, it is impossible to offer a unique logical characterization of the three clauses under study. In one instance, the three clauses are subjects, in another, they are objects. Indeed, one finds in both Poutsma and Jespersen a considerable proliferation of such mappings. Poutsma, for example, refers to adverbial clauses of place, time, cause, reason, consequence, inference, purposes, concession, disjunctive concession, quality, attendant circumstances, degree, alternative agreement, proportionate agreement, restriction, and exception.[2] In each case of adverbial modification, Poutsma observes the three types of clauses as being an instance of any single logical constituent. The most that Poutsma could say was that the three constructions are instances of "clause." This alternative presents several difficulties that we shall examine shortly. It is immediately clear, however, that this classification, regardless of any other deficiencies, asserts that there is no grammatical relation whatever between the clause and the noun. These entities are logically related insofar as they can play the same role in the sentence, but where it is possible to say with assurance that two items have the grammatical properties of nouns or clauses, there is no grammatical property that both nouns and clauses share.

In many cases, Poutsma's classificational scheme leads to analyses which, in terms of the earlier presentation, seem to be substantially correct. For instance, "that" clauses in sentences like "I think that John should go" are analyzed as objects of the verb. In effect, this coincides with the earlier analysis in which the NP dominating "it that John should go" is interpreted as the object of the verb "think" in the underlying phrase structure configuration. Similarly, the infinitive and gerundive phrases in sentences like "I swore never to divulge our secret" and "I suggest gaining permission first" are correctly analyzed as verbal objects. The major problem in Poutsma's analysis arises from the fact that his clausal analysis of the three complement constructions is taken overly seriously. Clauses, Poutsma hypothesized correctly, are actually sentences embedded in other sentences and they thereby perform some logical role. But it is the property of all sentences that the subject is in the nominative case while the object is in the accusative case. It follows, therefore, that a phrase such as "him to do that" in the sentence "I would like him to do that" could not be an instance of an infinitive clause, the reason being that the clause is a sentence and all sentences have nominative subjects. Thus, in the sentence "I would like him to do that" it is only the infinitive phrase "to do that" which is the clause. The pronoun "him" is actually the object of the sentence. This reasoning led Poutsma to postulate the so-called "accusative with infinitive" construction where the infinitive could modify the object or the subject. In other words, the complement constructions in "I caused him to go" and "I wanted him to go" are identical. Furthermore, the infinitive clause is, in each case, said to modify the object. It is also interesting that in sentences like "I would hate for him to do that" the "for" is claimed to be a preposition in the prepositional phrase "for him" while "to do that" is, of course, an infinitive phrase modifying the object of the prepositional phrase.

We see then that for every infinitival construction where a noun, pronoun, or nominalization intervened between the main verb and an infinitive clause, the same analysis was given, this analysis being similar to the verb phrase complement analysis discussed earlier. This comparison is, perhaps, a bit lenient since the assumption is being made that no special force should be attributed to Poutsma's insistence that the infinitive in accusative with infinitive constructions modifies the object. In any case, difficulties enough confront Poutsma's analysis. For example, can it be that the two sentences "I want John to go" and "I want to go" represent distinct constructions? The former is an accusative with infinitive construction while the latter consists of a verb and an infinitival clause as object. This would appear to be the case. At one point,[3] Poutsma suggests that when the accusative is a reflexive pronoun it is dropped after some verbs. But this assertion is of little help since it

ultimately says nothing more than that there is really no such thing as
an infinitive as object construction since it could be argued that the
reflexive pronoun is dropped in every case.

Jespersen's nexus theory constitutes an attempt to remedy the difficulty
Poutsma finds himself in. Unfortunately, this effort is a perfect instance
of throwing out the baby with the bath water. Nexus is "a combination
implying predication and as a rule containing a subject and either a verb
or a predicative or both. Besides these a nexus may contain one or more
objects, often a direct and an indirect object."[4] The application of this
view to the complement system is effectively summarized by Jespersen
in the following fashion:

> If we compare the following sentences,
>
> (1) they judged me a happy man
>
> (2) I believe him as honest as myself
>
> (3) this will make her happy
>
> (4) they elected Tom their chief
>
> (5) he slept himself sober
>
> (6) I want this done at once
>
> (7) I believe him to be an honest man
>
> (8) this will make the watch go
>
> (9) I want this to be done at once
>
> and if we ask in each case what is the object of the verb, many
> grammars say that in the first six it is the word placed immedi-
> ately after the verb, and the rest is called a "complement" of the
> object, or an "adjective or noun used predicatively of the object"
> (Sonnenschein); in the sentences (7) to (9) some writers speak of
> the infinitive as one of two objects.
>
> The correct analysis is that all these are analogous and contain not
> two objects (as in "I gave (made) her a ring"), but only one, which
> is a nexus containing the same two parts as a nexus that forms a
> complete sentence or clause; compare with (2) "I believe that he is
> as honest as I" and with (8) "this will have the effect that the watch
> goes." In (5) it is particularly easy to see that it is wrong to look
> upon the first part (himself) as the real object of slept: the result
> of his sleeping is that he became sober ("himself").[5]

Jespersen can be taken as asserting that the mere fact that a pronoun
following the verb in infinitival constructions must take the accusative
case is insufficient evidence on which to discard the clausal analysis for
infinitival constructions. Since the accusative case is the property of any
pronoun following a verb and can be explained with no reference to the
logical constituency of the pronoun, there is no reason whatever to
assume that the noun "Tom" in sentence (4), for instance, is not actually
the underlying subject of an infinitival clause taken as object. But where
Jespersen's view avoids the inconsistencies observed in Poutsma's anal-

ysis, it is accompanied by a host of other difficulties. First, it now becomes extremely difficult to offer a coherent explanation of infinitive clause subject deletion. Why should it be the case, for example, that the subject is deleted in "I want to be a virtuous man" but not in "I believe myself to be a virtuous man"? Why should it be that the sentence "what I want is to be a virtuous man" is grammatical but the sentence "what I believe is myself to be a virtuous man" is not? In preserving the clausal analysis to the exclusion of such constructions as Poutsma's accusative with infinitive, Jespersen effectively forfeited the ability to explain a wide range of differences which seem to accompany simple nexus constructions. He can and does list a good many of these differences, but never considers very seriously the possibility that they might actually have an explanation.

In fairness to both Jespersen and Poutsma, it must be pointed out that the sort of explanation whose absence is being claimed was not simply the issue involved in traditional linguistic analysis. It is difficult for the contemporary linguist to keep this in mind since both Jespersen and Poutsma say so many things that are either right or close to being right. For instance, both linguists recognized the phenomenon referred to earlier in this text as extraposition. That the sentences "it is strange that John left" and "that John left is strange" are related by an implicit rule was not doubted. Both of them recognized that prepositions are often suppressed before infinitival and "that" clauses; for instance, "I am aware of John's being honest" and "I am aware that John is honest." One can cite many instances of such insights. But the fact remains that these insights are the result of attempts to determine the way in which parts of speech, which, for all purposes, seem to include such entities as clauses as well as words, perform logical functions in the sentence. Thus the "that" clause in "it is strange that John came" performs the role of subject even though it is not in the normal subject position. Since the "that" clause in "I am aware that John is honest" performs exactly the same logical function as the gerundive clause in "I am aware of John's being honest," preposition suppression is a logical consequence. The fact that traditional approaches to complementation contain so much that is appropriate is a testimony to the goals of traditional description. But it seems no tribute to the traditional grammars to assert that certain of their results are confirmed by research in transformational grammar since one can hardly agree with the postulates that lead to these results. Furthermore, it is just these postulates that lead to so many false conclusions. In sum, the traditional grammarians did not use the data to get at the facts.

It is quite true, as both Poutsma and Jespersen thought, that clauses may play the role of an object in a sentence containing a transitive verb. But it is not the case, as both imply, that noun objects differ from clausal objects. This was a necessary conclusion, however, in a descriptive system which postulated a logical constituency rather than a grammatical constituency for sentences. Both clauses and nouns could be objects, subjects, and many other things, but the traditional grammarians found no way to express this generalization. It is automatic in a description that posits a grammatical constituency for sentences, since we may say that both nouns and clauses are instances of noun phrases and whatever affects a noun phrase affects both nouns and clauses. Thus we see that, in this case, the traditional grammarian who posits that a "that" clause may be an object of a verb is giving a correct observation for the wrong reason. A noun phrase may be the object of a verb, and insofar as we can prove that noun phrases may dominate "that" clauses, such clauses may be interpreted as verbal objects.

When Poutsma devises the accusative with infinitival analysis for a class of constructions, we find that his judgment is correct in many cases; for instance, "I defied John to go," but for entirely the wrong reason. The validity of this analysis has nothing to do with the accusative form of the noun following the verb but rather with a variety of considerations raised earlier in this study. Poutsma's formulation is incorrect as often as it is correct and, once again, for reasons which his view of linguistic inquiry could not offer. Similarly, Jespersen's nexus hypothesis produces the right analysis for a small class of items, but not for any reason which he proposed. And the analysis fails in so many cases, in the sense that nexus covers so wide a range of different phenomena which have merely superficial similarity that it becomes extremely difficult to think of the few correct instances as supporting the traditional approach to the phenomenon of predicate complementation. It thus seems inadvisable to devote further consideration to specific aspects of the traditional analysis of complementation. The traditional grammarians were extremely diligent. They present much data that are quite relevant to the construction of a grammar for the complement system. But a traditional approach could not provide such a grammar.

The most extensive treatment of the phenomenon referred to in this study as noun phrase complementation is found in Lees' The Grammar of English Nominalizations.[6] Lees correctly identified "that," "for-to," and "POSS-ing" clauses as instances of noun phrase complementation, but he was more concerned with the role played by such strings in the derivation of complex nominal structures than with the various underlying structures and transformations required to handle complementation in general. Lees' work is extremely insightful, and it is pertinent to discuss those aspects of his discussion of nominalization that are relevant to the present study.

The noun phrase complement constructions discussed in this study are instances of what Lees calls "factive" nominals and "action" nominals. Sentence (1) is an instance of the former while sentence (2) is an instance of the latter.

(1)   for him to have eaten vegetables was a great surprise

(2)   to eat vegetables is healthful

In this discussion of factive nominals, Lees clearly recognized the necessity of an extraposition transformation, a preposition suppression transformation, and a generalized transformation that embedded the nominal into a noun phrase. Certain features of Lees' discussion are not quite right however. In his analysis of the passivization of "complement-type" sentences such as "he was persuaded to work," we observe that he assigns a verb phrase complement analysis to the active form. In other words, "X persuaded Y to work" has the structure NP-AUX-V-NP-S. As we have seen earlier in this study, there is considerable justification for the analysis in which the phrase "to work" is an instance of a noun phrase complement dominated by a prepositional phrase. Lees' analysis was probably conditioned by Chomsky's early work in which verb phrase complementation was assumed to be a more productive phenomenon in English than it actually is.[7]

One of the most interesting aspects of Lees' analysis concerns the formulation of a "second passive" transformation to handle the derivation of sentences like (3).

(3)   a.   they were believed to have seen him

    b.   he was thought to be rich

In Lees' analysis, the second passive transformation operates on a string like "I think that he is rich" to generate the string "he is thought to be rich by me." Lees was forced to postulate this additional transformation since the "regular" passive must apply to the highest level NP to the right of the verb in the phrase structure. Thus, the regular passive would always yield the string "that he is rich is thought by me" and never "he is thought to be rich by me" since the pronoun "he" is necessarily dominated by a higher NP. We now know that the passive sentence "he is thought to be rich by me" does arise through the application of the regular passive transformation, at least in part. The passive transformation produces the string "it for he to be rich is thought by me." Through the application of two independently motivated transformations, the extraposition transformation and the pronoun replacement transformation, we generate first "it is thought by me for he to be rich" and second "he is thought by me for to be rich." Applying the second complementizer deletion transformation, we derive the string "he is thought by me to be rich." It thus appears probable that Lees' second passive transformation is unnecessary.

In his discussion of gerundive nominals, Lees raises an interesting question concerning certain types of restrictions apparently imposed upon the subject of the complement sentence. Consider, for example, the following:

(4)   a.   1.   swimming there is great fun
         2.   *his swimming there is great fun

    b.   1.   dressing oneself is fun
         2.   *dressing himself is fun

Lees suggests that these restrictions may have something to do with the "action"-"factive" distinction, but they may also be explained by certain more general considerations. We observe that "fun" may take a prepositional phrase, as in (5).

(5)   a.   swimming there is great fun for him

    b.   swimming there is great fun for somebody

It is abundantly clear that the subject of the complement sentence is the same as the noun phrase in the prepositional phrase.

(6)   a.   (his) swimming there is great fun for him

    b.   (somebody's) swimming there is great fun for somebody

Now let us suppose that in these constructions, as in all cases of verb phrase complementation, identity between the subject of the complement sentence and the noun phrase in the prepositional phrase is obligatory. Since these two noun phrases are connected, it follows that the identity erasure transformation, which also must apply, will erase the subject of the complement sentence, giving the sentences in (7).

(7)   a.   swimming there is great fun for him

    b.   swimming there is great fun for somebody

Finally, we know that pronominals like "somebody" can be deleted, giving thereby sentence (8).

(8)   swimming there is great fun

We see that sentence (8) can have only one source: both the subject of the complement sentence and the noun phrase in the prepositional phrase are "somebody." Furthermore, since the identity erasure transformation is obligatory, sentence (4a. 2) is automatically blocked. If the noun phrase in the prepositional phrase in the underlying structure for this sentence had been "somebody," then the identity erasure transformation would have been blocked. Since the noun phrase was "he," the grammar correctly generated (7a).

These same considerations explain the restriction on (4b. 2). It is clear in this sentence that the underlying subject of "dressing himself" must have been "he." Thus sentence (4b. 2) is blocked for exactly the same reason as (4a. 2).

Not all of the restrictions Lees raises can be handled in this manner however. Consider the following:

(8)   a.   eating vegetables is fashionable

    b.   *his eating vegetables is fashionable

There is no obvious independent motivation for postulating an underlying prepositional phrase analysis in this instance, although this possibility is not entirely out of the question. In any case, insofar as the action-factive distinction does not offer a reasonable explanation for the fact that the subject of the complement sentence in (8a) can and must be the unspecified pronoun "somebody" to the exclusion of everything else, one suspects that a deeper explanation will be forthcoming. Yet short of stating that "fashionable" is an adjective that requires an unspecified pronominal subject in the underlying structure of the complement sentence, the considerations raised in this study seem to offer little help.

An examination of a few of Lees' analyses lead one to suspect that he

overlooked certain relevant facts. Thus, for instance, one finds Lees
assigning a common derivation to such pairs of sentences as (9) and (10).

(9)   the man is reluctant to go

(10)   the man is clever to go

As we have seen earlier, however, there are a great many differences
between these sentences. Consider the following:

(11)   a.   1.   it is clever of the man to go
           2.   to go is clever of the man

       b.   1.   *it is reluctant of the man to go
           2.   *to go is reluctant of the man

These data suggest that sentence (10) does not have the same derivation
as (9) but rather something quite different. Perhaps, as suggested
earlier, the derivation of (10) depends upon the application of the pronoun
replacement transformation. This could not, however, be the case for (9).

With respect to sentences (12) and (13), Lees correctly points out the
similarity between what we have called verb phrase complementation
and the complementation observed in these sentences.

(12)   he is willing to leave

(13)   he is free to leave

There is little question that sentence (13) is an instance of verb phrase
complementation, but it is not at all clear that the same may be said for
(12). Consider the sentences (14):

(14)   a.   1.   I am willing for you to leave whenever you are ready
           2.   what I am willing for is for you to leave whenever you are
               ready

       b.   1.   *I am free for you to leave whenever you are ready
           2.   *what I am free for is for you to leave whenever you are
               ready

The cost of insisting that sentence (12) is an instance of verb phrase
complementation is that of losing the generalization that all verb phrase
complement constructions require obligatory identity of the connected
noun phrases. Furthermore, to the extent that (14a. 2) is grammatical, it
is clear that sentence (12) is a noun phrase complement construction and
that the complement originates in a prepositional phrase in the underlying structure. Thus there is considerable virtue in asserting that these
two sentences are not the same.

One could point to several other instances similar to (14). Their enu-
meration seems a little beside the point since it is perfectly clear that
my criticisms of Lees' work imply nothing more than that he sometimes
overlooked relevant data. The general adequacy of his theoretical framework is not at issue.

What the present study tells us is that it is not the transformational machinery by which noun phrase complementation differs from verb phrase complementation. Indeed, the set of transformations required in the derivation of these constructions is the same for both. The only difference between the two resides in the underlying structure produced by the phrase structure rules. The major burden in the grammar of the predicate complement constructions falls, therefore, not on the transformational rules but on the phrase structures rules, in particular PS Rules 1 and 2, which produce the full range of predicate complementation in English.

Fillmore's work[8] on complementation is less extensive than Lees' but interesting nonetheless since it was Fillmore who first directed serious attention to complement sentence markers. His discussion of the telescoped progressive is particularly noteworthy. On another topic, however, Fillmore overlooked certain critical facts and was led to an analysis that is quite suspect. In Fillmore's analysis of the verb "believe," for instance, he postulates that sentence (15) has an underlying structure in which the noun phrase "the butler" is verbal object.

(15)   the detectives believe the butler to have been murdered

Fillmore never discusses the considerations that lead to this formulation of an underlying structure, or, in his terms, the two terminal strings that are combined through an embedding rule to generate (15). It is thus difficult to say much beyond simply asserting that the proposed structure of the two terminal strings in this instance fails on two grounds. First, this formulation does not permit us to relate the sentence (15) with (16).

(16)   the detectives believe that the butler was murdered

Second, the analysis leaves us without an explanation of the synonymy of the sentences in (17) and the nonsynonymy of the sentences in (18).

(17)   a.   the detectives believe the butler to have been murdered by the cook
        b.   the detectives believe the cook to have murdered the butler

(18)   a.   the detectives forced the DA to interrogate the butler
        b.   the detectives forced the butler to be interrogated by the DA

These facts are explained automatically on the assumption that the sentences in (17) are instances of noun phrase complementation while those in (18) are instances of verb phrase complementation. Under these analyses, the nonsynonymy of the sentences in (18) is predicted from the fact that the underlying verbal object in (18a), "the DA," is different from the underlying verbal object in (18b), "the butler." In (17), the verbal object is the entire noun phrase complement construction, and the only difference between the two sentences is that the passive has applied to the complement sentence in (17a) but not in (17b).

This historical summary does many injustices to both the traditional and transformational linguists. The work of both groups warrants more intensive study. But the general characteristics of both approaches become fairly clear even on a cursory examination. The traditional approach to the study of predicate complementation is one of description without justification. The transformation approach, on the other hand, is one of description with justification where the essential goal is to explain successfully the data exemplifying predicate complementation. The present work is in the latter tradition and can be construed as confronting earlier transformational descriptions of predicate complementation with new data. In this sense, the rules proposed in the present study do not represent a grammar of English that differs in any crucial respect from earlier formulations in the transformational tradition. Rather, the present study constitutes a new synthesis of the rules in an adequate English grammar, and it differs from earlier formulations only insofar as it succeeds in providing an account of a new collection of syntactic phenomena.

Notes

1. R. B. Lees, "Transformation Grammars and the Fries Framework," in H. B. Allen, ed., Readings in Applied English Linguistics (New York: Appleton-Century-Crofts, 2nd ed., 1958), p. 137.

2. Hendrik Poutsma, A Grammar of Late Modern English (Groningen: P. Noordhoff, 1904), pp. 433–533.

3. Ibid., p. 576.

4. Otto Jesperson, A Modern English Grammar on Historical Principles, IV (New York: Barnes and Noble, 1956), p. 5.

5. Ibid., p. 7f.

6. R. B. Lees, Grammar of English Nominalizations (The Hague: Mouton, 1960), especially Chapter 3.

7. Noam Chomsky, "A Transformational Approach to Syntax," in A. A. Hill, ed., Third Texas Conference on Problems of Linguistic Analysis in English (Austin: University of Texas, 1962).

8. C. J. Fillmore, "The Position of Embedding Transformations in a Grammar," Word, 19, pp. 208–231.

Appendix. Verb Classifications

The lists in this appendix provide classifications of English verbs in terms of the complement structures in which particular verbs may participate. The lists are representative but by no means complete.

A.1 Object Noun Phrase Complementation

A.1.1. "that" complementizer

accept	deny	hint	point out	require
acknowledge	deplore	hypothesize	preach	represent
admit	desire	imagine	predict	reveal
advocate	discern	imply	prefer	rumor
affirm	disclose	indicate	prescribe	say
allege	discover	infer	presume	see
announce	dislike	insinuate	profess	sense
answer	divulge	insist	promise	specify
appreciate	doubt	intimate	pronounce	state
ascertain	dream	intuit	prophesy	stipulate
assert	emphasize	know	propose	submit
assume	estimate	learn	prove	suggest
believe	expect	like	postulate	suppose
certify	explain	love	realize	surmise
charge	fancy	maintain	reason	suspect
claim	fear	mean	recall	swear
comment	feel	mention	reckon	teach
complain	figure	mind	recognize	testify
confess	find	mutter	recollect	theorize
confide	foresee	neglect	recommend	think
conjecture	forget	note	regret	tolerate
contend	gamble	notice	reiterate	understand
decide	gather	object	remark	verify
declare	guarantee	observe	remember	wager
decree	guess	order	reply	write
deduce	hate	own	report	
demand	hear	perceive	request	

A. 1. 2.   "for-to" complementizer

1.   optional extraposition

bear	dislike	hate	loathe	prefer	require
demand	expect	intend	love	prescribe	want
desire	fear	like	promise	request	

2.   obligatory extraposition

acknowledge	conjecture	know	represent
admit	consider	maintain	show
affirm	declare	perceive	state
assume	deny	presume	suppose
attest	fancy	proclaim	suspect
believe	grant	pronounce	think
concede	guess	prove	understand
conceive	hold	realize	
conclude	imagine	recognize	
confess	judge	remember	

A. 1. 3.   "POSS-ing" complementizer

abhor	deride	justify	reconsider
admire	disavow	like	regret
advocate	discredit	love	relish
allow	discuss	mind	remember
avoid	dislike	miss	repudiate
await	dread	neglect	renounce
bear	endorse	notice	resent
cherish	endure	overlook	resist
consider	entail	pardon	ridicule
contemplate	eschew	postpone	risk
countenance	evaluate	praise	savor
criticize	examine	preach	stand
curse	fear	preclude	suggest
defend	forget	prefer	survive
denounce	glorify	protest	value
deny	hate	publicize	veto
deplore	imagine	question	vindicate
deprecate	intend	recommend	welcome

A. 2   Subject Noun Phrase Complementation

A. 2. 1.   intransitive verbs

1.   "that" complementizer

appear	matter
came to pass	seem
happen	turn out

2.   "for-to" complementizer

appear	seem
chance	turn out
happen	

A. 2. 2.   transitive verbs — all complementizers

alarm	comfort	exasperate	pain
amaze	compliment	exhaust	please
anger	concern	exhilarate	relieve
annoy	deafen	fluster	sadden
appeal	defame	frighten	satisfy
arouse	delight	gall	scare
astonish	fascinate	gladden	shame
astound	depress	gratify	sicken
attract	disconcert	harm	soothe
awe	discourage	hearten	startle
baffle	disgrace	help	stupefy
bedevil	disgruntle	horrify	suit
befuddle	disgust	humble	surprise
beguile	dishearten	humiliate	sustain
bemuse	dishonor	hurt	tempt
benefit	dismay	insult	terrify
bewilder	displease	interest	torment
bolster	disquiet	irritate	trouble
boost	dissatisfy	madden	unnerve
bore	distress	mortify	unsettle
bother	disturb	nauseate	upset
calm	elate	nettle	worry
charm	embarrass	outrage	
cheapen	enchant	overawe	
cheer	enrage	overwhelm	

A. 3   Intransitive Oblique Noun Phrase Complementation

A. 3. 1.   "that" complementizer

admit (of)	decide (on)	pray (for)
ask (for)	hope (for)	rejoice (at)
conceive (of)	insist (on)	wish (for)

A. 3. 2.   "for-to" complementizer

ache (for)	consent (to)	persist (in)	succeed (in)
aim (for)	decide (on)	plead (for)	thirst (for)
arrange (for)	hope (for)	plot (for)	wait (for)
aspire (to)	look (for)	pray (for)	wish (for)
beg (for)	long (for)	strive (for)	yearn (for)
care (for)	lust (for)	struggle (for)	

A. 3. 3.   "POSS-ing" complementizer

approve (of)	elaborate (on)	plan (on)
arrange (for)	engage (in)	pore (over)
bank (on)	escape (from)	protest (against)
beware (of)	gamble (on)	provide (against)
blush (at)	gloat (over)	puzzle (over)
boast (about)	gloss (over)	react (against)

brag (about)	guard (against)	rebel (against)
check (on)	harp (on)	reflect (on)
comment (upon)	indulge (in)	rejoice (at)
conceive (of)	inhere (in)	reminisce (about)
consent (to)	inquire (into)	scoff (at)
concentrate (on)	insist (upon)	slur (over)
cope (with)	intrude (upon)	sneer (at)
correspond (to)	jeer (at)	subsist (on)
count (on)	joke (about)	succeed (in)
decide (on)	know (about)	talk (of)
delight (in)	laugh (at)	think (about)
depend (on)	long (for)	weary (at)
disapprove (of)	muse (on)	wince (at)
dispense (with)	participate (in)	wonder (about)
dwell (upon)	persist (in)	write (about)

A. 4 Transitive Oblique Noun Phrase Complementation

A. 4. 1.   "that" complementizer

advise NP (of)	inform NP (of)	remind NP (of)
apprize NP (of)	notify NP (of)	tell NP (of)
assure NP (of)	persuade NP (of)	warn NP (of)
convince NP (of)	reassure NP (of)	

A. 4. 2.   "for-to" complementizer

advise NP (of)	drive NP (to)	persuade NP (of)
coax NP (into)	entice NP (into)	remind NP (of)
coerce NP (into)	force NP (into)	warn NP (of)
convince NP (of)	notify NP (of)	

A. 4. 3.   "POSS-ing" complementizer

absolve NP (of)	discourage NP (from)	prevent NP (from)
accuse NP (of)	dissuade NP (from)	prod NP (into)
bully NP (into)	entice NP (into)	prohibit NP (from)
cajole NP (into)	exclude NP (from)	provoke NP (into)
caution NP (about)	fool NP (into)	remind NP (of)
coax NP (into)	force NP (into)	save NP (from)
coerce NP (into)	goad NP (into)	scare NP (into)
convict NP (of)	lecture NP (about)	suspect NP (of)
cure NP (of)	pester NP (into)	trick NP (into)
deter NP (from)		

A. 5 Intransitive Verb Phrase Complementation

A. 5. 1.   "for-to" complementizer

begin	continue	fail	manage
cease	dare	get	proceed
commence	decline	grow	refuse
condescend	endeavor	hasten	start

A. 5. 2.   "POSS-ing" complementizer

cease

commence

complete

continue

finish

quit

recommence

A. 6.   Transitive Verb Phrase Complementation

A. 6. 1.   "for-to" complementizer

admonish	command	help	order
allow	commission	impel	permit
appoint	compel	implore	predispose
assist	defy	incite	prompt
bribe	detail	induce	schedule
bring	direct	inspire	stimulate
beseech	empower	instruct	tempt
bestir	enable	invite	train
cause	encourage	lead	trouble
challenge	enjoin	let	trust
charge	entreat	make	urge
choose	exhort	motivate	warn
coax	force	oblige	

A. 6. 2.   Progressive

apperceive	find	pass
behold	glimpse	perceive
catch	keep	see
detect	notice	show
discern	observe	watch
feel	overhear	witness

A. 6. 3.   "POSS-ing" complementizer

imagine

picture

remember

visualize

(There is virtue, perhaps, in asserting that a sentence like "I imagine myself being tall" is an instance of object noun phrase complementation along with "I imagine that I am tall." This assertion requires, however, that we allow extraposition for "POSS-ing" complementizers. Although we find cases where complement sentences containing "POSS-ing" are extraposed from sentence initial position, as in "it is useless trying to do that," such extraposition is not, in general, possible in sentence initial position. Subsequent research may show, however, that vacuous application of extraposition is possible everywhere for all complementizers, in which case the above classification will have to be revised.)

A. 7   Oblique Verb Phrase Complementation

bank (on)
impose (upon)
presume (upon)
prevail (upon)
rely (upon)

Index